Letters to a
SERIOUS
Education
President

Letters to a SERIOUS Education President

Seymour B. Sarason

CORWIN PRESS, INC.
A Sage Publications Company
Newbury Park, California

For information address:

Corwin Press, Inc.
A Sage Publications Company
2455 Teller Road
Newbury Park, California 91320

SAGE Publications Ltd.
6 Bonhill Street
London EC2A 4PU
United Kingdom

SAGE Publications India Pvt. Ltd.
M-32 Market
Greater Kailash I
New Delhi 110 048 India

Printed in the United States of America

Library of Congress Cataloging-in-Publication Data

Sarason, Seymour Bernard, 1919-
    Letters to a serious education President / Seymour B. Sarason.
    p. cm.
    ISBN 0-8039-6063-8. —ISBN 0-8039-6064-6 (pbk.)
    1. Education—United States—Aims and objectives. 2. Educational change—United States. 3. Education and state—United States.
    I. Title.
LA217.2.S27 1993
370'.973—dc20
92-37817
CIP

FIRST PRINTING, 1993

Corwin Press Production Editor: Marie Louise Penchoen

In Appreciation of

May 22, 1943

and

September 2, 1954

I

November 2000

Dear Mr. President:

Yesterday's results make you the first president elected in the twenty-first century. Given my very advanced age, I am delighted to be alive to wish you well. But, again because of my age, I feel compelled to do more than to convey my sincere wishes for a productive presidency. During the recent campaign you eloquently expressed two things: your frustration—frankly, bewilderment would be a more appropriate term—that past efforts to improve our schools have, generally speaking, failed, and, second, your explicit resolve and hope that you will truly be a more successful "education president" than any of your predecessors, save Thomas Jefferson. In one of your campaign speeches you said,

> Improving our schools is not an important problem, it is *the* problem because the survival of our ideals is at stake. In his inaugural address Franklin Roosevelt, faced as he and the nation was with the catastrophe called The Great Depression, said that we have nothing to fear but fear itself. I must tell you that today, as well as for the past half century, we have not been as fearful as we should be about the deterioration of our educational system. We have been concerned but not fearful, certainly not fearful to the point where we have been willing to say that we must have the courage to admit that we have identified the enemy and it is us: our past ways of thinking, our temporizing, our resort to quick fixes, our belief that somehow the nightmare will end and we will wake up to see a better day. My predecessors

1

were well-meaning people, but it is obvious that good intentions, like love, are not enough. And neither is money. If money is the answer, should not the billions we have poured into our schools have had some discernible positive effects? If instead of billions we had expended trillions, would our educational problems have disappeared or dramatically lessened? I wish I could say that the answer is yes or even maybe. Money was not the answer to The Great Depression, World War II was. As president I will not wait for the equivalent of a war to forge a new, more effective educational system. The moment of truth has arrived. Let us greet the moment honestly, courageously, inventively, in full awareness of the failures of our past ways of thinking and acting.

Those were stirring words, even to someone like me who long ago gave up hoping that our political leaders knew (or even wanted to know) what the educational game and score were. More correctly, that even if they *knew* the game and score, would they have the will to lead the nation in truly new directions . . . even though they, like Franklin Roosevelt and Harry Truman, would be called, in certain quarters, blind radicals, or bleeding heart liberals, or betrayers of national values, or utopian fools?

May I be so bold as to say that you may not be aware of the full extent of your kinship to Franklin Roosevelt. In his campaign for the presidency in 1932—the Great Depression was in its early stages—he ran on a platform that had two major policies: to reduce and to balance the federal budget. In short, his diagnosis of the causes of the economic breakdown was monumentally in error. It was not that he was a fool but rather that he, like everyone else, simply underestimated the dimensions and complexity of what was happening. It was not until he assumed the presidency that he began to comprehend how wrong his diagnosis and policies had been. Like you, he then gave us stirring words that heralded the New Deal era. And, again like you, he told the nation that past ways of thinking and acting were no longer adequate. He had the will, and he engendered that will in the nation, to take bold actions. What is the relevance of this for your presidency? Let me put it bluntly: Nothing in what you have said about our educational problems contains your diagnosis of what we are faced with. You have said all of the right things about past failures and our head-in-the-sands stance. It is to your credit that you have put education at the top of your agenda. Given all that has happened in the past decade, you clearly have convinced most people to support the priority you have given to education. But a priority is not a diagnosis. In this instance what I mean by a diagnosis begins with the recognition that we are not dealing with *a* problem and *a* diagnosis but a truly bewildering array of problems. If you do not know that now, your overwhelming moment of truth is not far off. What you should fear is not fear itself but the sense of being so overwhelmed by complexity that you substitute action for thinking. How will you decide what is a primary or "basic" problem? How prepared are you to resist the pressures to adapt this or that "solution," especially from quarters that, however well intentioned, have been part of the problem? Are you prepared to say loud and clear that you, we, are not faced with problems that have "solutions" in the way that four divided by two is a solution?

I confess that there is one absolutely crucial point about which you have said nothing and, therefore, that warns me not to be taken in by your inspiring words. Let me put my reservation in the form of a question. How clear is it in your head that you should have two overarching *moral* obligations: *to repair and to prevent?* It is only a slight exaggeration to say that up until now the emphasis and funding have been on repair, not prevention. Inevitably, they are interrelated, but the thinking that informs the repair effort is very different from that which informs efforts at primary prevention. You were correct to say that it was World War II that got us out of the Depression, i.e., that the repair efforts of the New Deal were inadequate. What I hoped you would go on to say is that the one piece of New Deal legislation that not only was a radical departure from our past but also the most successful was the Social Security Act. Undergirding that landmark legislation was the primary prevention way of thinking, i.e., to prevent the personal and social catastrophes of undue dependency in one's later years or in periods of unemployment. I am sure you agree with me on that point. But have you thought through what that means for how you will approach educational problems? What balance will you try to maintain between repair and prevention?

Friends tell me that there are more productive ways I can spend my remaining days than writing to you. For one thing, they tell me, it is wildly unrealistic to expect that a president can have other than a superficial knowledge of education in general and schools in particular. Instead of writing to the president I should find out who his educational advisors are and write to or meet with them. Better yet, they say, I should try telling the president from whom he should *not* seek advice and give him a list of people he *should* consult. Obviously, I have not heeded their counsel, and for a reason I shall get to in a moment after I have expressed the major doubt I had about writing you.

Presidents, I have concluded, are not readers. That may sound strange because a good deal of a president's time is spent reading more memoranda and reports than there are hours in the day. Indeed, a president depends on his staff to give him summary reports about reports, ending with options to consider for the purposes of action. Whatever a president reads has gone through a filtering or screening process. He assumes that what he reads contains the "guts" of a problem and the alternatives for action available to him. So why say that presidents are not readers? I say it for several reasons. First, reading summaries of summaries is no substitute for grasping the complexities of problems. Problems, *important* problems, are not only horribly complex but they have a history of errors of omission and commission that, if you are ignorant of them, makes it likely you will repeat those errors. No one, least of all me, expects you to bone up on the history of all important problems. But I do expect that that is precisely what you should feel obliged to do about a problem, in this case education, that you have put at the top of your agenda. To the extent that you depend on summaries of summaries, to the extent that you do not feel *compelled* to familiarize yourself with this problem, to the extent that you do not have the *curiosity* truly to read, to sample, in the literature on education, you are very likely to pursue courses of action that end up proving that the more things change the more they remain the same. Or, as with education, the more they get worse.

Franklin Roosevelt, Harry Truman, and John Kennedy were readers. They had a sense of history, better yet, a respect for history. They did not view history as a museum of relics to which you go on a rainy Sunday. I confess that nothing I have read about you suggests that you are a reader, that you will not be satisfied to "see" education only in terms of summaries of summaries. I hope you prove me wrong. Why anyone would want to be president of the United States has long mystified me. In many ways it is an impossible job. We are used to hearing that the presidency is the most powerful office in the world. I assume you have read enough to know that by the time a president leaves office he (someday it will be a she) is the world's expert on the constraints on the office. In regard to education you will find many constraints: constitutional, political, economic, and institutional. Those constraints are real, strong, and trying. But there is no constraint on articulating a vision, and by that I do not mean the mouthing of cliches, pious generalizations, and empty rhetoric. In fact, one of your major obstacles in improving our schools is that many people believe the situation is hopeless. No one has given them reason to hope, once again, that we are moving in new, challenging ways. No one has given them a compelling basis for believing that someone is, finally, getting at the heart of the problem. Far from being hopeful, people are resigned to a hostile apathy. No one has made them think. No one has clearly posed for them the hard choices they must think about. No one has reinvigorated, or even articulated, a sense of national mission. The people are wise, not jaded. Their stance is: We have heard it all before, why should we listen again? They know something is wrong. They are waiting for a new vision that will have the ring of truth, the ring that says: Yes, *that* is what we have forgotten, *that* is what we have to take seriously, *that* we must act on come what may.

So what should you read? I attach a small list of books. I hope that you will not view it as a display of hubris on my part that a couple of my books are included. They are there not because I have ever said anything new but because they contain the ideas of several writers you should take most seriously. Indeed, if the pressures on your time permit you to read only one book on that list, it should be the one by Alfred North Whitehead. He was no bleeding heart liberal or mindless reactionary. He was a philosopher, a stellar logician-mathematician who understood two related things: the nature and force of children's curiosity, and the ways that curiosity is too often blunted or extinguished in class-rooms. That is to say, he understood the differences between productive and unproductive contexts for learning. What Whitehead understood gets to the heart of the matter: how to sustain the boundless curiosity of very young children who leave their "wonder years" for years in the classroom. Many other writers have said the same things. And that is the point you must not allow yourself to forget: The core problem has long been identified. There is no great mystery here. Our past failures inhere in the inability or unwilling-ness to take it seriously. Inability or unwillingness may be inappropriate characterizations. It may be more correct to say that there has been a lack of leadership to give people a vision of what we would have to do if we took these things seriously. What you have thus far said publicly is not a vision but an expression of your resolve, your concerns, your hopes. In times of threats to our national security a presi-dent has no difficulty rallying people around our flag. The threat is concretely there, the people know it, they are willing to do whatever is necessary to repulse the threat. The people know *it*, and the recognition of *it* does not follow a Madison Avenue campaign of persuasion. In the case of education—which, as you have said, is as serious a threat as a foreign enemy to our security—no one has defined the central prob-lem, the *it*. If people know anything, it is that in response to the educational crisis there have been many "its" and many failures. The American people are neither niggardly nor stupid. In the case of education today it is as if everyone is from Missouri. They want to be convinced and so they ask: Where is the beef? Why should we get our hopes up again?

This letter is much longer than I intended. I initially thought I would convince you that you know far more about the important problems in education than you realize. Indeed, I was going to urge you to refrain from undue dependency on experts. You will have need for experts, but their value to you will be determined by how conscientiously you first look into *your* experiences as a student. You do not regard yourself as an expert, but I will try in my next letter to convince you that in an important way you *are* an expert.

I have not introduced myself to you and that was deliberate. Who I am, what I have done, what I have written should be of no importance to you. I know that sounds strange, if not ridiculous. My plea to you is to read this and subsequent letters with one question in mind: Do these letters have the ring of truth? I shall not, I assure you, present you with "data": statistics, graphs, research data, commission reports, etc. If sheer volume of *valid* knowledge were necessary and sufficient, we would not be in the morass we are. I have read that your favorite musical is *Guys and Dolls*. You will recall that delightful song "Adelaide's Lament" wherein she concludes that medical explanations of her psychosomatic upper respiratory colds are for the birds because they do not get "where the problem is": her single, unmarried status. What I shall endeavor to demonstrate in these letters is that in the case of our educational problems we have not dealt with where the problem is.

Between now and your inaugural you will be quite busy. But I do hope that you will find it in your self-interest to read my letter. It will certainly brighten my remaining days if you were to respond, however briefly, to anything I write. I confess I entertain the thought (fantasy?) that what I will say to you is very important for you and our country. It may be a delusion of grandeur on my part to believe that if you take what I say seriously, you will not end up as a footnote in future history books but with pages describing your courage to give the American people a basis for *re*educating themselves about the purposes of American schools. Our country has two kinds of history. One celebrates our traditions, values, and accomplishments. The other catalogues our departures from what we have stood for and should have done. You have the opportunity to lead this country in ways that will justify celebration and not add to the litany of our failures.

Respectfully,

Seymour B. Sarason
Professor of Psychology Emeritus
Yale University

P.S. Before writing this letter I assumed that I would not write a second one until I received a reply from you. I have changed my mind for two reasons. The first is that it is unrealistic to expect you to reply "promptly." You are swamped with the details of planning, selecting staff and cabinet, and ordering your priorities. The second is more personal but no less realistic: I am understandably aware that my days are numbered and that I should devote what energies I have to doing what I enjoy most, which is thinking and writing. So at varying intervals I will be sending you letters. But I do hope that at some not-too-distant week I will hear from you.

II

Dear Mr. President:

I assume that you do not consider yourself an expert on education but that you are expert in choosing and listening to people with new ideas. Put another way, you have confidence in your ability to distinguish between those who are giving you old wine in relabeled bottles and those who are giving you a new, bracing brew. In this letter I shall try to convince you that you have more than a little expert knowledge about a fundamental educational problem.

A Greek philosopher said, "The fox knows many things, but the hedgehog knows one big thing." One of our best observers of the human scene, Isaiah Berlin, put it this way in his book *The Hedgehog and the Fox*:

> . . . there exists a great chasm between those, on one side, who relate everything to a single central vision, one system less or more coherent or articulate, in terms of which they understand, think, and feel—a single, universal, organizing principle in terms of which alone all that they are and say has significance—and, on the other side, those who pursue many ends, often unrelated and even contradictory, connected, if at all, only in some *de facto* way, for some psychological or physiological cause, related by no moral or aesthetic principle; these last lead lives, perform acts, and entertain ideas that are centrifugal rather than centripetal, their thought is scattered or diffused, moving on many levels, seizing upon the essence of a vast variety of experiences and objects for what they are in themselves, without, consciously or unconsciously, seeking to fit them into, or exclude

them from, any one unchanging, all-embracing, sometimes self-contradictory and incomplete, at times fanatical, unitary inner vision. The first kind of intellectual and artistic personality belongs to the hedgehogs, the second to the foxes.

That, you will agree, is a helluva long sentence, but it serves the purpose, my purpose, of defining what I mean by a vision: a central idea, a big idea, that radiates out and magnetically attracts and interconnects a lot of other ideas. When I say that I am a hedgehog, or that someone else is, it does not automatically confer validity on their big idea, even though hedgehogs have no doubt that their big idea is right on target. Like it or not, you are hoist by your own petard. By virtue of the fact that you have put education at the very top of the national agenda, you will ultimately be judged by how good a hedgehog you were, how clearly you articulated a central idea, the flag around which you rallied the people. Your predecessors were foxes, they had no big idea. I do not say that to disparage them—some of history's most important people have been foxes—but rather to indicate that they did many things to improve education that were basically unrelated to each other. Parts remained parts. Some called it a crazy quilt approach. That's wrong because a crazy quilt has *one* purpose: to keep you warm in bed.

Lyndon Johnson was a partial exception. If you go back, as you should, and read his justification for Head Start, you will find his one big idea, his vision: Disadvantaged, impoverished preschoolers had the intellectual and personal capabilities to exploit and benefit from schooling if appropriately stimulated contexts were made available to them. They had all the marbles, so to speak, but no context in which to use and develop them. Provide them with that context and they will stay in the race. It was a morally inspired idea informed by a belief in the potential of these children *and* in the superiority of preventive over repair efforts. Why do I say that President Johnson was a "partial" exception? Because his vision of what children were and needed focused on the preschool years and wrongly assumed that when these preschoolers entered "real" school the context of learning would be no less stimulating, enriching, and productive. If the results of Head Start are encouraging but by no means dramatic, it is because his big idea was not big enough to alert him to the characteristics of most classrooms, to lead him to say: "What preschoolers want and need are what *all* students want and need, but our classrooms are not providing it because they are intellectually and personally frustrating and uninteresting places. What we owe these youngsters before they come to school, we owe to them *and everyone else* once they are in school."

Enough of this academic-professional preface! Professorial habits are not easily overcome. So forgive. I promise you no more quotations.

You and I grew up in very different worlds, and we come from very different socioeconomic, religious backgrounds. Despite all of the obvious ways we differ, I shall make the assumption that in one crucial respect we are very similar. Frankly, I would say we are, were, identical. Therefore, let me pose a question I shall answer in terms of my preschool experience, an answer I have no doubt you will find true for your early life. The question is: What stands out in your mind when you recollect what your preschool years were like?

What comes to my mind is that I was agonizingly aware that I did not understand most of what was happening in my circumscribed world. That is putting it negatively. The fact is that I had more questions about things, people, and happenings than anyone in my family could answer, even if they had been aware of the extent of my questions. It was not that my parents would not respond to my questions but rather that I rarely felt satisfied by their answers. Please do not conclude that I was a frustrated little kid whose parents did not "understand" him or, worse yet, were not interested in "stimulating" my mind. On the contrary, my Jewish parents (and grandparents) never let me forget that I had a "head" I was obligated to use and develop so that when I entered school I would do well. More correctly, even better than well! And that meant that I would not have to struggle as they did in an America in which they were fearful, very unsophisticated immigrants. If asked how they instilled in me a need to achieve, I truly cannot tell you. It's like my learning to like the ocean and to swim in it: It was before I entered school, and it had to be under the tutelage of my father who was quite a swimmer.

If my parents could not satisfy my curiosity, or were unaware of all the questions I had that went unasked and unanswered, they at least did nothing to cause me to give up the myriads of internal questions I had about myself, people, and their relationships. Why is the sky blue? What makes an automobile move? Why is my sister's body not the same as mine? Why does my grandfather have a beard and my father does not? Why do my grandparents talk in a language (Yiddish) I do not understand? What is Yiddish? Why do my parents argue with and even holler at each other? Why should I be afraid of "goyim": Italians, Irish? Where is Manhattan? What is Manhattan? Who is Babe Ruth? Why is money so important, and why doesn't my father have more of it, why does he have much less than my aunts and uncles? What happens when a person dies? Where is heaven? Who is God? What is a school? What is a dream? How does steam come up from the cellar to our apartment on the sixth floor? How is rain made? Snow? How come a telephone rings, you put the receiver to your ears, and you hear a voice? Why don't we have a telephone? Why does an aeroplane stay in the sky? Why does heat make water boil? How does a clock work?

The fact is, Mr. President, that those early years are truly years of wonder, awe, fascination, and bewilderment. That was true for me, for you, and for every biologically intact preschooler. Even if you believe that newborns vary in their genetic-intellectual endowment, that belief in no way invalidates the fact that they are quintessentially question-asking organisms who, if their questions are ignored or not answered, come up with their own answers. You can no more stop this internal or external question asking than you can stop the ocean tides. You can restrict, inhibit, and even punish this question asking when it is articulated, but you cannot extinguish it. It may go "underground," it may impoverish the desire to explore. It may have all kinds of consequences that negatively affect the pursuit of learning, but question asking is too built into the human organism to be extinguished.

There is no doubt that parents of very young children vary dramatically in their comprehension of the significance of question asking. It is far beyond the purposes of these letters to suggest how we can productively improve that comprehension. But it is my purpose to tell you that too many educators do not grasp the big idea that what fuels productive intellectual development are question asking and answers that then engender new questions.

I have observed scores of preschool programs (Head Start and others), and I have found very few that have taken that idea seriously. They are very well intentioned in that they seek to give children opportunities to work with interesting and stimulating materials, to learn how to be with other children, and to experience a personal sense of competence. These are laudable goals that some programs, by no means all, achieve. But with very few exceptions these programs view these youngsters as if they come with no burning desire to understand themselves, others, and the world. These children are asked to conform—and it is a requirement—to what adults consider interesting and important. What they, the youngsters, have experienced and are experiencing in their lives—the questions they have, the puzzles that stimulate or plague them—are rarely a focus. They are supposed to think and do what others say they should think or do. That is why I consider these programs adult and not child centered. To be child centered means, to me at least, that you start where children are: what they bring, what they think, what they want to know and learn. They have what is called an "inner life" and that is what you start with. Yes, they seek new experience, but they also seek answers about themselves, others, and the world.

You don't ask a president to spend a few mornings observing preschoolers. But that is what I do ask you to do so that you can determine for yourself whether what I have said—what you and I can recall about our preschool days—is true: That however interesting these programs are to children, they are not geared to the concrete questions children have. Unlike me, you were in a preschool program. To what extent did your preschool program provide a forum that allowed *your* questions, *your* concerns to surface? Your children were in preschool programs, as my daughter was. Were you as struck as I was about how much that was on her mind, and on the minds of all children, rarely surfaced in her preschool program? Some, perhaps you, might ask: Is a preschool program supposed to be a substitute for the parental role of comprehending, eliciting, discussing what are to children puzzles, questions, concerns? Of course not. But it does not follow that these programs should produce a gulf in the minds of children between what they are asked to think and do in the program and what they think and do when they are "alone with their thoughts." That gulf, Mr. President, not only mammothly increases when children start "real" school, but for many children, rich and poor, that gulf becomes unbridgeable. Two unconnected worlds.

Am I making too much of the centrality of question asking in human development? Is it a big idea that can be carried too far? Perhaps, but I doubt it. What cannot be doubted, what research has conclusively demonstrated, is that the preschool child possesses all of the intellectual characteristics of the budding scientist and artist: the capacity to ask questions, to seek answers, to doubt, and to explore. Yes, children need a lot of things from those who care for them. They do not need to be taught to ask questions. That is built into the human organism and is quite obvious in children long before they have acquired language. Humans are curious from their earliest days. Nurturing that curiosity is our most important obligation and task. We discharge that obligation very poorly as parents and educators.

I have been in the game too long to expect that you will not have *questions* about the big idea. I do expect that on reflection you will agree with much that I have said. Your questions, if I am right, will be about more practical matters. You are a man of action. You will want to know what you should *do* consistent with the big idea. But before you think in terms of action, you will have to ask *and* answer a question: Why has the big idea not been taken seriously? I shall answer that question, albeit too briefly, in my next letter.

Needless to say, my self-appointed task would be easier and certainly more interesting if I knew what was going on in your mind. I do not like being in the position of too many teachers who follow a curriculum that their students find uninteresting and irrelevant to what concerns them, i.e., their "other" world.

Our greatest presidents were not simply men of action in the narrow sense. They were individuals possessed by a vision they sought to convey to the people. Putting, as you have, education at the top of your agenda is a decision, not a vision. What is the big idea you want the American people to accept and, therefore, to be willing to support? That is why I ask you to ask why the big idea has not been taken seriously. How you answer that question will determine whether what you convey to our citizenry is an assemblage of cliches or a galvanizing vision.

Respectfully,

Seymour B. Sarason

P.S. I hope that you do not take my remarks about preschool programs as being unduly critical. In no way did I mean to suggest that they are without merit. Candor requires that I say that a fair number of those programs perform a baby-sitting role competently, and that is about all they do. It will only be when you have, as I have, observed programs informed by the big idea that you will understand why I say what I do. And you will understand why I would despair if you defined action primarily in terms of increasing the number of programs, personnel, and budgets. Doing that is the easy way out, the quick-fix approach. It's like depending on sand bags to contain a roaring, swollen, ever rising river. Just as money cannot buy you happiness (the usual exceptions aside), it cannot buy the goal of capitalizing on and exploiting the productive, creative, self-motivating capacities of children.

III

Dear Mr. President:

I await patiently a reply to my letters. I have become quite knowledgeable about the physical frailties associated with advanced age, but I am grateful that I can still think and write. Therefore, I shall continue to write to you. It adds meaning to my (few) remaining days. I find it amusing that I regard you as my wife, Esther, regards me: someone who needs to be protected from himself. My hope is that you will come to see that much of what I write has the ring of truth and that it will not take you years to hear it. It took me years—after much kicking, screaming, resisting—to admit that my Esther was right far more often than not. So, if I have reached an advanced age, it is because I finally allowed myself to hear that ring of truth. Yes, Mr. President, I am a hedgehog who thinks he is right on target. And, yes, you have to become a hedgehog in regard to what you have put at the very top of the national agenda. America today needs a hedgehog, not a fox. Now to the question I asked you to ponder: Why has the big idea not been taken seriously?

There are many perspectives from which human history has been written. It is not surprising that the one that fascinates me describes how difficult it has been for people to change their conceptions about human capacities. It is not happenstance, of course, that there has been an intimate relationship between the struggle for human freedom and changes in conception about what people are capable of becoming. Over the millennia the most frequent situation was one in which rulers viewed the ruled akin to cattle who needed and wanted to be told what to think and do. To the rulers their people were an undifferentiated mass each human atom of which had an undifferentiated "mind." I speak as if all that is in the past. As you well know, Mr. President, there are many places in the world today where that situation is all too obvious.

Why do we continue to be astounded by the early Greeks? How do we explain them? Thousands of books have tried to answer that question and thousands more will be written. If our explanations still leave us with mystery, there are things about which we are certain. One is that these early Greeks asked questions—about the world and the human mind—never asked before. It is as if the shackles on the human mind disappeared and the questions poured out, questions for which answers gave rise to new questions in the tradition of science where the more you know the more you need and want to know. No society, *then or now*, had such *respect* for the human mind, *all* minds. Not only the minds of rulers but the ruled as well. The other thing we know is that the Greeks took seriously the idea that everyone had the obligation and capability to participate in ruling. For me the Greek "lesson" is that how you regard the human mind is never logically separable from how you nurture that mind. And that, Mr. President, is as true for what happens in a classroom as it is in the society at large.

The history that fascinates me is a history of the struggle against the underestimation of the capabilities of the people. I trust you are aware that in our national history there has never been an immigrant group that was regarded as other than intellectually stupid, culturally barbaric, and a source of pollution in the body politic. And what about the capabilities of women? Of Blacks? Of old people? Of handicapped people? We have a national history of which we should be proud, but that pride should not blind us to how we have been victims of underestimating the capabilities of people. We like to believe that we are no longer victims of that tendency. If that is true, how then do you explain why you have been forced to put education at the top of the national agenda? Clearly, I assume, you did not do that because you believe that school children are incapable of learning and thinking better than they do. You believe that they *are* more capable than educational outcomes indicate. You *know* that they are not being "reached." You *know* that too many of them have not been turned on but rather turned off by schooling. And there is one other thing a moment's reflection will tell you you know: When you observe these turned-off youngsters—both in our inner cities and suburbia—*outside* of schools, they are active, motivated youngsters seeking to understand themselves, others, and their world. They have curiosity, questions, and creativity in regard to matters or goals you and I may not like. We would want them to be more interested in ideas, history, literature, and science, but they are not. Why not?

One reason is that in our well-intentioned but misguided efforts to pour information into the minds of children we are rendered insensitive to what *their* interests, concerns, and questions are. Let me put it this way: Although we know that much is in their heads—they do think, feel, fantasize, and strive—we regard what is in their minds as unimportant, or irrelevant, or (worse yet) as an obstacle to what *we* want *them* to know, feel, and strive for. We do not *respect* what is in their heads, i.e., they are not thinkers, they have unformed minds that are up to us to form. It is as if our job is to clean out their Augean mental stables. How can you take seriously people whose minds you regard as unformed and chaotic? What is there to get out of them? Empty heads need to be filled! The fact is—and it is a fact, Mr. President—that children, even very young children, have minds that are organized, stamped with purpose and curiosity.

There is a second reason that is no less fateful. *In practice* we regard children as incapable of self-regulation, unconcerned about or ignorant of the rules of social behavior, as organisms one step above (if that) of animals or cannibals. Give them an inch and they will demand a mile. Trust them to be responsible and you will regret it. Open up the sluice gates of "permissiveness" and you will drown. Give them their "head" and they will take your body. My words may strike you as caricature, but please remember that caricature is a way of emphasizing a truth. In this instance the truth is that we regard children as in need of taming.

When you put the two reasons together we have a situation characteristic of our classrooms: "*Where* students are" is ignored and "*what* students are" is something we should fear and, therefore, tame or extinguish. As a result, we have classrooms in which students are passive, uninterested, resigned, or going through the motions, or unruly, or all of the above. It is a classic case of the self-fulfilling prophecy, i.e., we begin with invalid assumptions and then act in a way that "proves" their validity.

I have to ask you this question: Do you react to what I have said as if I was an advocate of a mindless permissiveness that assumes that if you let children be "where and what they are" they will find their own ways to values and goals you and I cherish? That if we get out of their way, they will do the right thing in the right way, as if they possess a kind of wisdom we who teach them do not? If you, like many people, react in these ways, it is because you have not had the opportunity to test your assumptions, thereby confusing assumption with empirical fact. *Sit in classrooms, Mr. President.* Make your own observations. Fairness requires that I tell you that there are classrooms in our public schools where teachers have taken the big idea seriously. Far from being chaotic or devoid of law or order, or a struggle between a well-intentioned teacher and passively aggressive, bored students, they are lively places where learning is pursued, where minds are active, searching, challenged. Please note that I did not say happy minds because true learning is and should be experienced as challenging, at times frustrating and puzzling but always energizing. Unfortunately, these classrooms are, relatively speaking, minuscule in number. The modal classroom is a boring, uninteresting place unconnected to the interests and questions of students. Forgive me for being repetitive. For these students there are two worlds: the isolated world of school and the "real world" of passions, personal needs, strivings, personal and social identity, and, yes, questions about what is, what should be, and what will be.

Back in the legendary sixties it became fashionable for college students to take a year off and go abroad. A wag quipped about one such student, "He went to Europe to find himself except he wasn't there." Well, Mr. President, young children begin school expecting to find themselves, but they end up disappointed.

If you take the big idea seriously, the educational task is quite clear: How do you capitalize on, exploit, direct, and interconnect "where and what children are" to bodies of knowledge and concerns that contribute to an examined life in which horizons broaden and a sense of historical identity is forged? In short, how do you bring the two worlds together? If we do not seek to enter their worlds, they will not seek to enter ours.

One of the books I suggested you read was *The Teacher* by Sylvia Ashton Warner, an account of how she went about teaching the native Maoris of New Zealand to (among other things) read. More correctly, how she *thought* about how to get these children to *want* to read. She did not regard these native children the way too many Americans view the capabilities of our natives, or Blacks, or Hispanics, or our poor, rural "hillbillies." Mrs. Warner had no doubt whatsoever that these Maori youngsters had active, curious minds. So what did Mrs. Warner do? She asked each child what words he or she wanted to learn, *not* what a predetermined "curriculum" said children should learn. It made no difference if the words concerned the body, sexual matters, or whatever. If they wanted to learn a word—which was then written on a card for them—that is what she helped them learn. And they learned! And at a pace and with a level of motivation she did not find at all surprising. She did have problems with the educational authorities! The important point, Mr. President, is that Mrs. Warner was a hedgehog whose central, big idea was that if you start with "where and what children are"—if you intellectually engage and hook them—you can then, and only then, help them want to acquire knowledge and skills that expand their horizons and options.

Mrs. Warner's book had, I think, the status of a best seller. Obviously, for many people it had the ring of personal truth. Unfortunately, for all practical purposes it had no impact on *our* educational practices. The perception of a truth does not necessarily make you "free."

In, I suppose, typical professional-academic style I have not given you a direct, persuasive answer to why we have not taken the obvious seriously. That was not evasion on my part, because I wished first to persuade you that you have to come to grips with where you stand in regard to "what and where children are." So in my next letter I shall try to be more direct and, I hope, persuasive. If I am persuasive, I predict there will be a part of you that will regret it.

Respectfully,

Seymour B. Sarason

IV

Dear Mr. President:

I do not write on this day to send you Thanksgiving greetings. Yesterday afternoon Esther went to the post office to mail my previous letter. As luck would have it, on the evening news last night they had an extended segment of your press conference at Dulles Airport prior to your taking off for a vacation. Esther, who is (among other things) an expert in these matters, remarked that you look terrible— "He looks as aged as you do," she said—and that if you continue the pace, you will not be alive to be inaugurated. As I indicated in an earlier letter, Esther's track record in regard to the consequences of a male's sense of physical invulnerability is unexcelled. No one needs to give her lessons on the superiority of prevention over repair. Esther is (was) a clinical psychologist, not a physician, but if you ever are in need of a second opinion, call her (203-248-2571)! I am being only half facetious. Esther takes a dim view of experts. "They wouldn't recognize a whole person if they met one." I give thanks on this holiday for my Esther.

What compels me to write you so soon after the previous letter is how you responded to this question by a member of the press: "Mr. President, you have put educational reform at the very top of your agenda, and the election results have to be seen as supportive of that priority. My question is: Can you give us some concrete idea of the direction you plan on taking? Where will you start and why?" Frankly, I expected you to give out with some cliches or unexceptionable generalizations. But you did not, thank God. You were not only concrete but personal, so personal (and with practically no reaction time) as to suggest that you are capable of using your personal experience to think about matters educational. According to the *New York Times* account of the press conference—fortunately I do not have to depend on my memory—you said the following, which I urge you to put on your desk in the oval office as a way of reminding yourself of a very important experience:

> Let me tell you about me and my first course in algebra. I was a good student and not only in algebra. Algebra came easily to me. But it was also very uninteresting and downright boring. I never understood and no one every bothered to explain why we had to learn algebra. Well, one day I screwed up enough courage to ask our teacher why we had to learn algebra. When I asked that question, the rest of the class broke out in applause. The teacher became visibly upset. He quieted us down and said that he wanted to finish the lesson for the day but that tomorrow he would try to answer the question. The next day he started the class by saying: "I am going to present you with two choices, and you have to decide which of the two you will choose. Keep your choice to yourself. The first is that on the first day of next month I will give each of you a million dollars. The second is that on the first day of next month I will give each of you a penny, on the second day I will double it, that will get doubled on the third day, and the doubling will go on for each subsequent day of the month. Think about it for a few minutes and make your choice." Everyone opted for the million dollars and, of course, we were shortchanging ourselves. He then went on to demonstrate the law of compound interest and the formula for it. To say that we were astounded is to put it mildly. All of us were interested in money, and I can honestly say that was a peak day in my school years. What I thought I knew was wrong. What I needed to know I now *wanted* to know, and the more the better. I shall ever be grateful to that teacher for how he made formulae important and interesting on that day. He was a superb teacher.

And that is where I plan on starting: Getting more teachers like the one I had in algebra.

That is a splendid example of the big idea: starting with a question or problem intrinsically interesting and relevant to the world of students, and if there is anything we can be certain about is that from early life children are interested in money. What is a bank? What is a check? Who prints money and why? Why do people save money? Why do some things cost more than other things? What is a tax? Why are there so many kinds of taxes? For young children money is not just money. It is a "something" the adults in their world talk about, many of them worry about, some have scads of, and others have none of. For children money is a difference that makes a difference in lives, although they are puzzled about the origins of those differences. Don't you find it strange that something that is a source of interest and puzzlement to children is for all practical purposes unexploited in classrooms as a way of understanding our world and theirs?

But (there is always the professorial but) your refreshingly illuminating anecdote raises some troubling questions. Why did you have "to screw up your courage" to ask a reasonable question? Why didn't you ask the question much earlier? Why didn't your teacher on day one give concrete examples of how something as abstract as algebra has, had, and will have countless applications in the real world of real people? Why was your teacher "visibly upset" by your question? Why did he feel he *had* to finish the day's lesson plan? Finally, Mr. President, *after* that peak day did he continue to connect algebra to your world?

I hope you do not see me as a carping critic who is only satisfied—and, therefore, always dissatisfied—when the criteria for perfection are not met. Although your anecdote illustrates the big idea, your conclusion, your *policy* for action, is a distraction from examining the implications of the anecdote. Of course we want and need teachers who can do what your algebra teacher did on that day. You did not, I hope, intend to convey the impression that we need teachers who will respond to the questions of students only when forced to by the courageous likes of you. Did you wish to convey the impression that what that teacher did on *that* day makes him a model of what teachers should be? Do you not wish that that teacher, and teachers of other subject matters, acted more frequently and consistently with the big idea? I have no doubt that your algebra teacher was *by conventional criteria* a "good" teacher, by which is meant that he understood algebra, i.e., its internal logic and development. But what your anecdote poses is *the* educational task: How to connect the world of algebra to the world of students in ways that do justice to both? And that task holds for algebra, physics, biology, history, literature, and a lot more.

So, when you say that you will seek to increase the pool of teachers who will be like your algebra teacher, you will pardon me if I say your conclusion about policy is a misguided one. You have had the courage to convince the American people that transforming our schools is the number one priority. No ifs, ands, and buts. I ask you to respect my resolve to be as direct with you as you have been with the country. Your anecdote parted somewhat the curtain hiding the big idea. Your policy for action narrowed the opening. But on this Thanksgiving Day I am thankful that the parting of the curtain has at least started.

Esther tells me that the feast is ready. The table is beautiful—with Esther and my daughter, Julie, that was inevitable—the food will be most tasteful, but a mite too nutritious for a hedgehog like me.

Respectfully,

Seymour B. Sarason

P.S. One quick fact. In the modal classroom in a modal period of forty-five minutes, the average number of questions asked by students is around two (in some instances it was one student who asked the two questions). Teachers asked questions in the range of 40-150. So much for the power of big ideas.

V

Dear Mr. President:

Forgive this belated reply to your letter. I got my annual major cold, despite flu shots, a lot of Vitamin C, and submitting to Esther's demand that I wear a heavy coat. Esther believes in the germ theory of disease. I don't.

There were two bright spots in this personally disastrous month. The first was hearing the joke about the legendary Claude Pepper, the congressman who a few decades ago did so much for the medical concerns of senior citizens like me. He went, of course, to heaven and was ushered into God's presence. He asked God if he could ask one question—I obviously take to *anything* about questions. The question was "Will the United States ever have national health insurance?" God became reflective, pondered the question, and finally said, "Yes, but not in my lifetime." I tell you this joke because transforming our so-called health system is your number two priority. Given your top two priorities, you would do well to adopt God's realistic time perspective, a necessity in light of what I shall say a little later in this letter.

Seriously, I am most grateful for your letter in which you promise to read my letters and personally to direct them to your educational advisors. I fully understand when you say that you will not be able to reply as frequently as you or I would like, but in no way should that stop the flow of letters to you. That means a lot to me. Knowing you will read what I write takes the edge off that feeling of loneliness associated with old age. I do not need or ask for sympathy. By virtue of having been a professor (but still "professing") I need and ask what all professors seek: an audience. And when my audience of one is the President of the United States, my cup doth runneth over!

I did not know that your wife had taught school for several years. I am delighted that you have shown her the letters and that she assured you that I was, far from being senile, saying things that needed to be said. Obviously, you, like me, somehow managed to pick the right kind of mate. The press describes your wife as "strong willed." You should, as I do, thank God for big favors. God forbid the press should say *anything* about whether what your wife says is right or wrong. I hope she continues *not* to know "her place."

I owe you an explanation because on rereading my previous letter I was aghast at my failure to give you a crucial reason why the big idea has never taken hold. It was not because of memory loss or professional absentmindedness but rather, I think, that I am writing about serious matters in the format of letters, whereas I am used to writing books, relatively unconcerned about whether I am taxing the reader's patience. I am, believe me, very sensitive to the countless demands on your time and, as a result, I find myself striving to be brief—too brief for me but, no doubt, not brief enough for you! Changing formats requires a kind of relearning experience the difficulty of which is almost always underestimated. And that fact brings me to what I omitted.

If you take the big idea seriously, you have to confront this question: How do you capitalize on and nurture children's curiosity and questions about themselves, others, and their social world? There is a related question: How do we connect those characteristics to issues, values, bodies of knowledge, and skills that we in the adult world consider necessary and desirable for productive living? How do you begin to connect the "two worlds"? And by connect I mean the forging of a seamless web containing both worlds.

Traditionally (and unfortunately) we have not started with these questions but rather with a predetermined answer. We have not started with "where children are and what they are" but with a highly differentiated, complex organizational structure in terms of age and the calendar, grades, curricula, testing, levels of educational authority and responsibility, and encapsulated classrooms in encapsulated schools. The rhetoric of what I call the culture of schools is organized for one, and only one, purpose: to further the intellectual and social development of children. And those who articulate that rhetoric are well-meaning people who truly believe that the structure and rationale of school not only can achieve their intended purpose but is the best way to do it.

But these good people also know that their intended purpose is not being achieved for the bulk of students. And that knowledge has always initiated a tinkering process, e.g., change the curricula, develop remedial services, involve parents, employ new technologies, beef up the preparatory programs for educators, and increase in-service training programs.

One thing these people know for sure: "We are not reaching these kids." What do they mean by *reach*? To me (and most people, I assume) to *reach* somebody implies that you seek to establish a basis for connecting your world and their world. When these people say they are having difficulty reaching kids, what they mean is "we cannot get them interested in *our* world." In practice—in the "real world" of schools—it is expected that students will conform to the requirements and purposes of the school world at the expense of giving expression to their world. So we have the situation where both students and educators know that there are two unconnected worlds.

What educators find so difficult to grasp is that they perceive students through the prism of an existing structure and rationale of a school that virtually guarantees that the big idea cannot be taken seriously. That is to say, they so unreflectively accept the rationale and structure as to remove the big idea from the arena of action and practice and place it in the arena of empty rhetoric.

What I am saying, Mr. President, is that educators—and not only educators—do not start with the question: How do we capitalize on and nurture the questions and interests of students? They start with a predetermined organization and rationale to which they require students to conform. That makes educators sales people, i.e., selling something in which customers are not interested. It's only a slight caricature to say that their basic approach is that of Henry Ford, who said, "You can buy any color Ford you want as long as it is black."

In one of your recent press conferences you were asked if you now see the world differently from the vantage point of the oval office. You were refreshingly direct and candid when you said that you had not fully recognized the implications of the size, structure, and complexity of the federal government. And you went on to say that it is all too easy for someone in the oval office to become so immersed in matters of structure and organization as to lose sight of purposes and goals. Your exact words were: "Yes, when you are in the oval office, the world looks very different and that has its pluses and minuses. The plus is that you better appreciate the complexities of structure and action. The minus is that all of the pressures work in the direction of maintaining the status quo. In the process of dealing with the means of governance you can forget the ends of governance." That, I can assure you, Mr. President, is a statement that earned you brownie points for entrance to heaven!

A school or school system is the smallest of organizational pygmies compared to the federal government. But the wisdom in your words holds for our schools: Once you become part of the structure, tradition, and their rationales, the big idea (*any* big idea) loses salience and compellingness. Socialization is the process whereby you become what others want you to become. There is nothing inherently wrong or evil in that. It is wrong and evil when that process has the effect of *disconnecting* an individual's personal goals and values from those of the organization. That is what happens to many educators and most students. They live in disconnected worlds.

The big idea represents the most direct challenge to the way schools are structured and organized. I am sure that in the course of reading this letter you have been asking yourself what the implications of that challenge are for action. You want me to be concrete, to indicate in practical terms what the big idea may entail. I shall try to do so in my next letter. In the meantime I urge you to ponder the following:

1. Do you really believe in a gut sense that children are curious about themselves, others, and the world around them, that they seek to absorb knowledge and skills that give them the sense that they are *willingly* changing?

2. Can that absorption process be productive if we do not start or take into account "what children are and where they are"? Can they enter our world if we do not enter theirs?

3. Are not 1 and 2 glimpses of the obvious, aspects of which have been known for centuries and some of which have the most solid basis in systematic research?

4. If your answers to 1, 2, and 3 are what I hope they are, are you prepared to spearhead the challenge to the way schools are?

Respectfully,

Seymour B. Sarason

VI

Dear Mr. President:

This will be short. I am aware that I have told you nothing about myself, on the assumption that who I am or have been, or what I have written, are less important than getting you to use your experience of schooling as a basis for the policies and actions you are considering. As I have said, you are not without knowledge about what makes education a productive experience.

Beginning in 1966 I began (orally, and in print) to express doubts about the effectiveness of the scads of programs (local, state, federal) intended to improve our schools. With each passing year my doubts were transformed into the certainty that these programs were well-intentioned but doomed. And that certainty in turn led to the conclusion that not only were these efforts doomed but that the situation would get worse. Unfortunately, Mr. President, I was right, which explains why you *had* to put education at the top of your agenda. Some might argue that I was right for wrong reasons, which is to say that the big idea is wrong. It is no indulgence of arrogance on my part to suggest that someone who has been 100% right in his predictions for more than three decades is not likely to be a utopian fool.

Respectfully,

Seymour B. Sarason

P.S. Your Presidents' Day card came today. It truly made our day. When we went to the polling booth on election day,

Esther, knowing me as she does, made me promise that I would vote for you. Given my state of health, the fact that it was raining very hard, plus my sense of pessimism that pulling the lever is a difference that could make a difference, I expected that Esther would tell me to stay home while she went to vote. But no, she bundled me up, put me under a big umbrella, and told me how to vote. When the results came in, it was obvious that *you* had *reached* a large majority of our nation. That was the night I decided to begin to write to you. I confess that the world took on a very different cast for me when I read on the bottom of the Presidents' Day card three words in your handwriting: "Please keep writing." I will.

VII

Dear Mr. President:

You plan, plan, plan and then something happens—an event, a memory—that upsets those plans. My plan—indeed my promise to you—was to indicate what it could mean to take the big idea seriously. I started to write to you and then memory took over, and in a way and with a force that made me not only tear up what I started to write but to go back on my word not to subject you to long quotations. Since I do not lightly break a promise, I ask your patience and forgiveness. My justification is two-fold: I want to impress on you that anything I have said or will say has been said by others long before I came on the scene, and the quotation is one that many people have found interesting and important. Please bear with me.

From the standpoint of the child, the great waste in the school comes from his inability to utilize the experiences he gets outside the school in any complete and free way within the school itself; while, on the other hand, he is unable to apply in daily life what he is learning in school. That is the isolation of the school—its isolation from life. When the child gets into the schoolroom he has to put out of his mind a large part of the ideas, interests, and activities that predominate in his home and neighborhood. So the school, being unable to utilize this everyday experience, sets painfully to work, on another tack and by a variety of means, to arouse in the child an interest in school studies. While I was visiting in the city of Moline a few years ago, the superintendent told me that they found many children every year who were surprised to learn that the Mississippi River in the textbook had anything to do with the stream of water flowing past their homes. The geography being simply a matter of the schoolroom, it is more or less of an awakening to many children to find that the whole thing is nothing but a more formal and definite statement of the facts which they see, feel, and touch every day. When we think that we all live on the earth, that we live in an atmosphere, that our lives are touched at every point by the influences of the soil, flora, and fauna, by considerations of light and heat, and then think of what the school study of geography has been, we have a typical idea of the gap existing between the everyday experiences of the child and the isolated material supplied in such large measure in the school. This is but an instance, and one upon which most of us may reflect long before we take the present artificiality of the school as other than a matter of course or necessity.

Though there should be organic connection between the school and business life, it is not meant that the school is to prepare the child for any particular business, but that there should be a natural connection of the everyday life of the child with the business environment about him, and that it is the affair of the school to clarify and liberalize this connection, to bring it to consciousness, not by introducing special studies, like commercial geography and arithmetic, but by keeping alive the ordinary bonds of relation. The subject of compound-business-partnership is probably not in many of the arithmetics nowadays, though it was there not a generation ago, for the makers of textbooks said that if they left out anything they could not sell their books. This compound-business-partnership originated as far back as the sixteenth century. The joint-stock company had not been invented, and as large commerce with the Indies and Americas grew up, it was necessary to have an accumulation of capital with which to handle it. One man said, "I will put in this amount of money for six months," and another "So much for two years," and so on. Thus by joining together they got money enough to float their commercial enterprises. Naturally, then, "compound partnership" was taught in the schools. The joint-stock company was invented; compound partnership disappeared, but the problems relating to it stayed in the arithmetics for two hundred years. They were kept after they had ceased to have practical utility, for the sake of mental discipline—they were "such hard problems, you know." A great deal of what is now in the arithmetics under the head of percentage is of the same nature. Children of 12 and 13 years of age go through gain and loss calculations, and various forms of bank discount so complicated that the bankers long ago dispensed with them. And when it is pointed out that business is not done this way, we hear again of "mental discipline." And yet there are plenty of real connections between the experience of children and business conditions which need to be utilized and illuminated. The child should study his commercial arithmetic and geography, not as isolated things by themselves, but in their reference to his social environment. The youth needs to become acquainted with the bank as a factor in modern life with what it does, and how it does it; and then relevant arithmetical processes would have some meaning—quite in contradistinction to the time-absorbing and mind-killing examples in percentage, partial payments, etc., found in all our arithmetics.

That was written by John Dewey in 1900, one hundred years ago! What is remarkable about that quotation is not only how cogently he describes the gulf between the "two worlds" but also how he identifies *a problem you said much about in your campaign speeches*: We have to do a better job of interesting children in math and science and, as a result, increase the pool of people desirous of a career in those areas. The present and past disaster in the teaching of math and science would not come as news to Dewey. So what is the point? You are a conceptual cousin to Dewey, but what you need to become is his brother, i.e., to see that the basic problem is how to interconnect two worlds kept apart in our classrooms. Any policy you will come up with that does not deal directly, courageously, and innovatively with that basic problem will be as feckless and wasteful as all past efforts. You can increase salaries, require would-be teachers to be more steeped in math and science, write new curricula—you can do all of these things and more but they will be of no avail if they are not based on and informed by the big idea: You start with and capitalize on the world of the students, their experience of and with their world, their questions, their curiosities, their puzzlements.

And now let me tell you about L.P. Benezet who in the twenties and thirties was superintendent of schools in Manchester, New Hampshire. You would have liked him, Mr. President, because he was a man of ideas, action, and courage. Several things bothered him no end. One was the ways in which elementary school kids (and teachers) struggled to master arithmetic skills. Indeed, the number of grade retentions due to the failure to master these skills was quite high. His concerns were based not only on studying data provided by school reports: He went into classrooms and observed, he took over classrooms, he interrogated students and teachers. The long and short of it was that he concluded, "The whole subject of arithmetic could be postponed until the seventh year of school and it could be mastered in two years study by any normal child."

Another thing that bothered him was the inability of students to explain their solutions to arithmetic problems in clear, intelligible English. In fact, he was appalled generally at the low quality use of English, written and oral. So he did the following, for which he deserved a Nobel Prize for gutsiness and imaginativeness.

In the fall of 1929 I made up my mind to try the experiment of abandoning all formal instruction in arithmetic below the seventh grade and concentrating on teaching the children to read, to reason, and to recite—my new Three R's. And by reciting I did not mean giving back, verbatim, the words of the teacher or of the textbook. I meant speaking the English language. I picked out five rooms—three third grades, one combining the third and fourth grades, and one fifth grade. I asked the teachers if they would be willing to try the experiment. They were young teachers with perhaps an average of four years' experience. I picked them carefully, but more carefully than I picked the teachers, I selected the schools. Three of the four schoolhouses involved [two of the rooms were in the same building] were located in districts where not one parent in ten spoke English as his mother tongue. I sent home a notice to the parents and told them about the experiment that we were going to try, and asked any of them who objected to it to speak to me about it. I had no protests. Of course, I was fairly sure of this when I sent the notice out. Had I gone into other schools in the city where the parents were high school and college graduates, I would have had a storm of protest and the experiment would never have been tried. I had several talks with the teachers and they entered into the new scheme with enthusiasm.

The children in these rooms were encouraged to do a great deal of oral composition. They reported on books that they had read, on incidents which they had seen, on visits that they had made. They told the stories of movies that they had attended and they made up romances on the spur of the moment. It was refreshing to go into one of these rooms. A happy and joyous spirit pervaded them. The children were no longer under the restraint of learning multiplication tables or struggling with long division. They were thoroughly enjoying their hours in school.

At the end of eight months I took a stenographer and went into every fourth-grade room in the city. As we have semi-annual promotions, the children who had been in the advanced third grade at the time of the beginning of the experiment, were now in the first half of the fourth grade. The contrast was remarkable. In the traditional fourth grades when I asked children to tell me what they had been reading, they were hesitant, embarrassed, and diffident. In one fourth grade I could not find a single child who would admit that he had committed the sin of reading. I did not have a single volunteer, and when I tried to draft them, the children stood up, shook their heads, and sat down again. In the four experimental fourth grades the children fairly fought for a chance to tell me what they had been reading. The hour closed, in each case, with a dozen hands waving in the air and little faces crestfallen, because we had not gotten around to hear what they had to tell.

Please note, Mr. President, that although Mr. Benezet did not articulate the big idea, it was precisely that idea that informed the experience of students in "oral composition."

I do not use the word politician in pejorative terms. To me at least, a politician has two kinds of related expertise: He or she is (or should be) sensitive to "where people are," and he or she knows how to develop a constituency to support action. You are a successful politician, and so was Mr. Benezet. When you made educational change the number one problem on the national agenda, you were giving expression to what most citizens felt in their heart of hearts. When Mr. Benezet began his experiment, he started where he felt he had, or could develop, a supportive constituency. He did not start with those schools where parents of children were highly educated and resistant to any meaningful change. Although we do not know for sure, it seems as if he did ultimately convince those parents to go along with him.

The important point, Mr. President, is that the big idea does challenge the status quo in a truly revolutionary way. It entails the antithesis of tinkering. Most people cannot think of schooling except in terms of grades each of which has a predetermined, step-by-step curriculum, each classroom of which has a teacher "teaching children," i.e., telling them what they have to learn, making sure that they do not take step two before they take step one, all for the purpose of socializing them into our adult world, unreflectively requiring them to keep their world where it belongs: outside. It hasn't worked, it isn't working, and it will not work.

John Dewey said this a century ago. Mr. Benezet said and wrote about it (in the journal of the National Education Association) sixty-five years ago. It reminds me of the joke of the two psychoanalysts at the end of the day in the elevator. The younger one looked weary and dispirited, the older one looked spry, eager, alive, and happy. "How come," asked the younger one, "you listen all day to your patients and you end up, unlike me, looking ready to meet the world? How can you listen all day and still feel the way you do?" To which the older analyst replied, "Who listens?"

The point is, Mr. President, that if you "listen" to the big idea, if you take it seriously, your life is not easy, to indulge in understatement. That is why I write these imploring, entreating letters to you. I do so not because I think you will have trouble grasping the big idea. That is the easy part of it for you. No, my concern is that it will not inform the policies you will seek to implement; that you will—despite your concerns and desire to change things—end up plugging holes in a sinking ship.

I will have more to say about this in my next letter. In closing let me confess something. I hope and trust that you will not regard it as arrogance on my part that I very consciously seek to become your teacher. And I seek that not because I regard myself as all that wise or knowledgeable, as someone who wants to *tell* you what to think or do. No, what I seek in my role as teacher is to find out "where you are" in regard to educational change, i.e., the questions in your mind, the types of knowledge you want to acquire, the puzzlements, the thoughts you have not expressed publicly. You, like everyone else, do not parade all of your thoughts and concerns publicly. Put in another way: Consistent with the big idea, I seek to find out "where you are coming from and where and how far you want to go." Believe me, it is easy for me to run off at the mouth and pour information and suggestions into you. I know where I am coming from. As a teacher, however, I have to start with where you are. And if I start there, I may not only be of some help to you, but I will learn something I did not know before. The big idea is a way of mutual understanding and learning.

Respectfully,

Seymour B. Sarason

P.S. If there is usually a but in any sentence I write, there is usually a postscript to my letters. This one concerns the great American philosopher, Groucho Marx, who asked: "Do you want to learn French in ten easy lessons or five hard ones?" That question is in principle quite appropriate to matters educational. The history of educational change is the history of easy answers. Up to now no one in the oval office has been able to face up to hard answers. If you do, then Groucho's question has to be recast: Do you want to effect change in a hundred hard lessons over the next fifty years or ten hard ones in the next ten years? (There are no easy lessons.) My answer in a later letter will, I think, surprise you. There is another joke that is appropriate here, but it is not a short one and this letter is longer than it should be. The joke can wait, although at my age those are famous last words!

VIII

Dear Mr. President:

Having used Mr. Dewey and Mr. Benezet to run conceptual interference for me, let me relate my experience in the legendary sixties. I spent two years, two to three days a week, in a hundred-year-old ghetto elementary school. Most of that time was spent in kindergartens and the first two grades. Briefly, what I observed was the manufacture of problems, especially in grades one and two as teachers sought to "teach" reading and numbers. At the end of the day the teachers were tired and dispirited and so were the children. Whatever buoyancy, eagerness, and interest the children displayed when they entered kindergarten was slowly but steadily extinguished by the end of the second grade. It was not that the teachers did not struggle valiantly to get the children to learn the alphabet, combinations, and words. The teachers were serious and devoted *to the curriculum*, which is not the same as saying that they were devoted to the children. They liked the children—who were very likeable and even lovable— but to these teachers these children were there to learn reading and numbers, period. That was when I learned about the gulf between the world of children and the world of the teacher-centered classroom.

In one of my meetings with these teachers I listened, for the umpteenth time, to their frustration about the pace of the learning of these children. "These kids are not ready to learn" was the frequent refrain. For reasons that are still by no means clear to me, I heard myself say to the teachers: "What if you did not *have* to teach reading and arithmetic? What if it was illegal to teach reading and numbers in the first two grades?" The teachers viewed that as a gift from God, as salvation for their frustrating professional existence.

They enjoyed the fantasies my suggestion (which I labelled as Sarason's Law) triggered.

After indulging their fantasies of educational heaven, one of the teachers asked: "But if we did not have to teach the curriculum, *what would we do with them?*" And with that question, Mr. President, the teachers steered the discussion back to their reality. I resisted their resistance by trying to get them to consider two questions:

1. What terrible misfortunes would befall these children *and* our society if Sarason's Law were passed?

2. Are there not many ways in which you can stimulate the minds of children that would be intellectually and educationally productive without being confined within a predetermined curriculum?

Even though no teacher could come up with a "misfortune," they made it clear they preferred to deal with their here-and-now frustrations. We never got to the second question. We went on to other matters.

The point is, Mr. President, that these teachers—like most everyone else—were so imprisoned by imagery of what *should* go on in a classroom that my suggestion could not be pursued. The role of the teacher, the obligations of students, the predetermined curriculum, learning determined by the calendar—with imagery and traditions like that, alternative conceptions (like the big idea) are viewed as products of a fantasyland, a kissing cousin to Disneyland.

Let me backtrack for a moment. My suggestion in no way was based on the conclusion that these children were stupid, or unimaginative, or unmotivated. I had observed many of these children when they entered kindergarten, and I had occasion to talk with them individually. I had also, because of other interests and responsibilities, spent time in their neighborhoods. The conclusion I had come to (slowly, somewhat inchoately, but compellingly) was that *their* world was vastly different than the world of school, and, I must emphasize, that did not mean that the former was inferior to the latter in ways that stir the mind. It was rather that the two worlds were *different*.

Nor was it the intent of Sarason's Law that it should apply only to ghetto schools. It was intended across the board as a way of beginning to counter the attitude among *children generally* that school is a place where you learn what teachers say you should learn even though it is uninteresting and unrelated to all that interests you. Of course there is much that we want children to learn but *not* at the expense of a *willing* pursuit of knowledge, skills, and understanding. It is that willing pursuit that gets extinguished in our schools. There are many students who have passed their algebra course whose memory loss for algebra occurs quickly. Algebra is (or can be) important, and so is memory loss! When will we begin to face up to two facts? The first is that learning anything unrelated to your quotidian existence is unproductive. The second is that attempts to make that learning productive, based as they have been on what *should* go on in a traditional classroom, have been ineffective.

Mr. President, you are hoist by your own petard. You *know* that something is radically wrong. In your press conference last week you were described as somewhat curt when, in answer to a question about your educational policy and programs, you said, "I am not ready yet to present legislation to Congress. The situation is too serious to permit me to come up with legislation before I feel confident we are not going to repeat the mistakes of the past. I am not going to act for the sake of acting. Too many of my predecessors acted under pressure. Let me just say one thing and then close this conference: When I do come up with a program, it is going to create a stir. When in 1954 the Supreme Court rendered their desegregation decision, it created a stir because it confronted the American people with the necessity of changing their attitudes, practices, and even lifestyles. Forty-seven years later it is still creating a stir. That should not have been surprising. I will create a stir, not because I will enjoy it but because a serious situation requires it."

When I read that I allowed myself fleetingly to believe that you are taking my letters seriously. I say fleetingly because too many times in the past your predecessors in the oval office ended up proving that they, like our schools, were subject to the criticism that the more things changed the more they remained the same.

To explain my attitude and to lighten (I hope) your day, I'll end with one of my favorite jokes. It is about the journalist assigned to the Jerusalem bureau of his newspaper. He got an apartment overlooking the wailing wall. After several weeks he became aware that regardless of time of day, there was this old Jew praying vigorously before the wall. There must be a story there, he concluded. So he went to the wall, introduced himself, and asked, "What are you praying for every day before the wall?" The old Jew looked at him somewhat puzzled and said, "What am I praying for? In the morning I pray for world peace. Then I pray for the eradication of illness and disease from the earth. I go home for lunch and then I come back and pray for the brotherhood of man." The journalist was taken in by what the old Jew said. "You mean that *every* day you come to the wall and pray for these things?" Yes, the old Jew said. "How many years have you been coming to the wall and praying for these wonderful things?" The old Jew became reflective and replied, "How long? Maybe twenty, maybe twenty-five years." The journalist was stunned. Finally he blurted, "How does it feel to be praying all those years before the wall?" To which the old Jew replied, "How does it feel? It's like talking to a wall."

I too am an old Jew, but I find it hard to pray.

Respectfully,

Seymour B. Sarason

IX

Dear Mrs. Third Lady:

Esther, my wife, is my first lady and Julie, my daughter, is my second. So assigning you third place puts you into a very select group of individuals. You will understand. What you have no reason to understand is that your letter created a problem between Esther and me. To say that I was over-joyed is really an indulgence of understatement. I was ex-cited, told Esther that I wanted immediately to write you and eat later (if at all), and began scurrying about for this and that book, this and that newspaper clipping. Scurrying is too strong a word although it felt as if I were scurrying like a youngster getting things together to go out and play ball. Esther read the riot act to me —she knows it by heart in three languages (English, Yiddish, and French)—ending with the decision that I would eat first, take my medication, take a nap, and then, and only then, could I write *a* letter to you. And if I wrote more than one letter, she would not mail it. We came to a compromise: I would do as I was told. I am captain of my fate and master of my soul!

My excitement was not because you sent me a letter but rather its contents. What is sweeter music to the ears of a writer than to learn that someone made it their business to read some of the books he has written?

You asked a number of questions and I shall attempt to answer each briefly.

1. Of course I do not mind your writing to me. I am delighted that your husband has passed my letters on to you. I certainly will not regard hearing from you as a brush-off from your husband. I accept without reservation your state-ment that your husband reads each of my letters and that the two of you discuss them. I find it both heartwarming and

even "antique" that the two of you have such a close relationship. The media describes you as "tough," a "someone who knows her own mind" or a "someone who is not a shrinking violet." Your letter confirms their descriptions in a most gracious way. It is relevant to what I have said in my letters to note how hard it is for the media—even some of the women in them—to give up longstanding views about wives of Presidents. Attitudes do not change quickly, but rather according to geological time. I remember well how the media derogated and satirized Eleanor Roosevelt. And they mightily resented Rosalyn Carter for not denying that she expected that she would discuss national issues and policies with Jimmy. The media seems to regard wives as teachers do students: They should know their place and role and keep hidden whatever individuality they possess. Enough of that sermon.

2. Yes, I will treat any letter I receive from you or the president as confidential. You requested that I treat such letters judiciously. I substitute confidential for judicious. It is rare these days that anyone asks my opinions or advice about anything. And, as my early letters indicate, I had to overcome a good deal of resistance to begin to write to your husband. I thought that I no longer had any axes to grind (i.e., to *want* to grind an axe), except, of course, with Father Time. Him I hate! He will win.

I have this moment decided that I should not answer your other questions *in this letter*. You asked some very important questions, especially those in regard to the abysmal school performance of Black and Hispanic children and to the social disturbances to which they are indirectly related. But precisely because I am writing to you and your husband, there are "messages" your husband in his literally unique role needs to convey to the nation. Please bear with me.

The first message is that there is no way our schools can become more effective except by sustained efforts *over decades*, especially if the effort is informed by the big idea. Let me illustrate what I mean by an experience I had in an aeroplane before there were jets (I go back a long way!).

It was on a flight from Idlewild (now Kennedy, of course) to Dallas. When we left the gate to taxi for ten minutes to take off, it became immediately apparent that the pilot was a frustrated disc jockey. Among other things, he told us that our "four Evinrudes" would get us off the ground and give us a smooth flight. He went on and on. We took off. I had a window seat. We had been flying for an hour or so when billows of smoke began to pour out of one of the motors. I struggled against incontinence. At which point the disc jockey came on to say: "Those of you on the right side of the plane can see that one of our Evinrudes is malfunctioning. We were aware that something was wrong ten minutes ago and we feathered the motor." He never explained "feathering," thank God. He went on: "We can fly to Dallas with three motors but it is against the policy of American Airlines. So, we will put down in Louisville." A couple of minutes later he was back on: "We will not put down in Louisville but in Cincinnati. Now when we get to Cincinnati, you will see scads of fire-fighting trucks lining the landing strip. That is standard operating procedure. We will, I assure you, land safely and smoothly." And we did. During the three-hour wait for another plane I saw the pilot and told him how scared (what a weak word!) I had been, conjuring up, as the smoke did, memories of early movies about World War I and flaming, plunging airplanes. He then said to me something I have never forgotten because it contained a principle that illuminated aspects of my thinking about changing school systems. "The only time you have to worry about these flying monsters is when you have to put them down *quickly*. You can't put them down *quickly*."

That principle holds in spades in regard to changing the thousands of our school systems, some of which are monstrous in size, each of which is administratively autonomous. Helping one individual change is no *easy* matter, and when you face the fact that a school system is a collection of individuals in diverse, direct, and indirect relationships with each other, and varying in age, years in the system, status, motivation, different stages of burnout, points of view, and more, change has to be reckoned in decades, not years. And, as you insightfully said in your letter, our schools should not be seen or understood apart from our colleges and universities that prepare educators. So, when we seek to change schools we cannot ignore higher education.

No president has ever asked the nation to confront a realistic time perspective in regard to educational change. In part that is because no president has truly grasped the big idea and its implications for action. They have seen the problem as an engineering one, much like the problems that have to be overcome to build a bridge or the problems we "solved" to permit us to get to and stay in outer space.

In part, past presidential failures have been political in nature! No president has had the courage to say to the people: "To change our schools will require decades, because you cannot change in a few years an institution and its ideological underpinnings that have existed for centuries." Assuming as past presidents have that such a message guarantees defeat in the next election, they opted to do what they could do, *not* what needed to be done. They miseducated the American people. They trusted the good sense of the people the way we trust and respect the ideas of school children. I may be too harsh and wrong here because I am assuming that past presidents had an inkling of what the game and score were. That assumption is shaky in the extreme. Your husband is the first president who "seems" to have an inkling, which is why I began to write to him. To your letter I would also say seem but without quotation marks.

Now for the second message, very much related to the first. Above everything else a president is an articulator of the American moral vision. That is to say, the task of a president is to remind people of their obligation to be true to the best of our ideals and moral values, to remind them that we are a country born by breaking with stultifying tradition, that we are obligated to do what we have to do come what may, that boldness in the face of impending disaster, military or otherwise, is an American virtue. The Civil War was fought to uphold the principle that states could not secede from the Union. The Emancipation Proclamation was a moral necessity. The GI Bill of Rights after World War II was the discharging of a moral obligation to those who served in the military, a piece of legislation that literally transformed our society. And the boldness of the Marshall Plan saved Europe and us. And what kept us going in the Great Depression was the moral leadership of Franklin Roosevelt. The great presidents were moral leaders who did not allow the people to forget what America was about and *had* to do.

As no previous president, your husband knows that if we do not radically change our schools—just as our founding fathers in 1787 knew the radical changes in governance they had to contemplate and propose—America will lose its moral justification for existence, its moral innards. I am far from being a super patriot. And, I assure you, Mrs. Third Lady, that I am quite aware of the times our country did not live up to the rhetoric of its moral charge.

I do not know how to put it any other way: Can your husband articulate a moral vision in regard to education that will get a commitment from the citizenry to take the long view out of moral necessity, and to give up unrealistic views based on the most unrealistic time perspective? Like the airplane in my story, our educational system has been and is malfunctioning. Unfortunately, more than one motor is spewing smoke.

This has not been an easy letter for me to write, a fact of which Esther has been aware and commands me to end. One more thing: Unless the moral vision is informed by the big idea *and* its implications for action, conditions will worsen.

Respectfully and Gratefully,

Seymour B. Sarason

P.S. I will not attempt to explain why some subsequent letters will be addressed to Mr. and Mrs. President. I am comforted (another weak word) by the knowledge that both of you read my letters. The next few days will be taken up with visits to an assortment of medical specialists and laboratories (God help me, because I don't think *they* will). But when I rest up from those visits I will answer the other questions you ask in your letter.

P.S. I keep telling Esther that a letter a day keeps the doctor away. Her standard reply is: "You are not capable of *just* writing a letter. You agonize about each sentence and you end up exhausted. And if we needed a doctor quickly, where would we get one? The wisest thing the Hegelian Woody Allen ever said is that not only God is dead but try to get a plumber on Sunday. One letter every other day, and that's that." You would love Esther. Not so incidentally, back in the sixties, Esther did what is still the *only* observational study of the teaching of what was then the new math. I learned more from her study about why reform efforts were doomed than from any other study. That is why in an earlier letter I urged your husband to observe classrooms. It is one thing to talk about education, it is quite another thing to observe it in action. Saying that in a letter to a former teacher is truly to bring coals to Newcastle. Even though Esther will read this letter, I have to admit I am exhausted, but most pleasantly so.

X

Dear Mr. and Mrs. President:

Why, you asked, has the gulf between the school performance of Black and Hispanic children, on the one hand, and
white children, on the other hand, continued and may even
have increased? Although I shall give you my answer, it is
the opposite of undue modesty on my part for me to say that
I do not see myself, and do not desire you to see me, as
someone who understands most, and certainly not all, of the
factors contributing to those disastrous findings. I have a lot
of strong opinions, not least of which is that I have limitations in experience, knowledge, and wisdom! I am a hedgehog, not a fox. I have one big (but simple) idea through
which I see the world of schooling. There have been times I
wished I was a fox who knew a lot about a lot of things. But
hedgehog I became, and hedgehog I shall die. I have *never*
walked into a library without experiencing despair at the
thought that I would never be able to read every book in it.
Why do I tell you this? As but another way of saying that
the most important goal of education is to support the desire
to learn as much as one can about one's self and one's world,
regardless of whether you are a hedgehog or a fox. There
are only a few things you can count on to sustain you over
the lifetime (e.g., love, family) and one of them is the desire
to understand yourself and your world. We know ahead of
time that not everyone will strive for that goal, but that is no
warrant for not trying our darndest to increase the number
of children who will have such a striving. The most grievous
mistake we have made is to start with the assumption that
young kids do not have such striving, that they are not by
nature explorers, question askers, and knowledge seekers. I
have been criticized as being at best impractical and at worst

an egregious utopian. That, let us remember, were the criticisms directed at those who started the "American experiment." And, needless to say, they were the criticisms directed at those seeking the liberation of women. Mencken once said that no one could go wrong *underestimating* the intelligence of the "booboisie." A lot of people have been very wrong and our schools reflect their error. I read to Esther what I have just written and she said, "Stop agonizing and sermonizing and answer their question." I will, but (always a professorial but) I have to start by saying something about an assumption implied by your question.

You are, I am sure, aware of the yearly polls about attitudes and knowledge in different age groups in our country. For the past decade, at least, those polls have found that those below the age of thirty, in contrast to older groups, have dramatically less interest in or knowledge of current affairs, e.g., politics in general, elections, voting, etc. Those appalling findings—which I intuited in the last decade before I retired in 1989—are based on population samples most of whom were white, not Black or Hispanic. There is no doubt that if in these samples we were able to make a white versus Black-Hispanic comparison in regard to educational performance, the former would have significantly higher scores than the latter. The point is that despite higher scores a frightening percentage of whites are *uninterested* in what goes on in the world. I do not place full blame on our schools—the explanation *is* more complicated, but neither do I exempt their schooling from criticism.

Your question seems to assume that the higher academic performance of whites is an unalloyed "good" we should seek for Blacks and Hispanics to attain. I would be the last to object to such seeking but I would be among the first to ask: At what expense to the life of the mind? Do we want Black and Hispanic youth to stay in school, to be graduated, and, like their white counterparts, end up having as much or less interest in and knowledge about themselves and the world? The gulf in school achievement between these groups is scandalous, but what is truly frightening (*not* too strong a word) is the degree of *disinterest* and *social ignorance* among young people in these groups. What we owe Black and Hispanic and other minority youngsters is what we owe white ones. What I object to is posing the question as if the higher educational performance of white youngsters implies that their test scores reflect the acquisition of social attitudes, usable knowledge and skills, and personal-intellectual satisfactions that give meaning and purpose to a life *and* the society in which that life is lived. Such an implication is at best a hope and at worst a fantasy, or, as the polls suggest, both. I have to repeat: it is unfair to place all of the blame on our schools. To the extent that they have not taken the big idea seriously, they deserve blame.

Back to Blacks and Hispanics. Let me start with some statements (opinions?) about ideas and proposals, some of which have come from the Black and Hispanic communities. Some of these statements are critical and controversial, but the situation is too serious and pressing to tread lightly, to avoid offense at the expense of candor.

1. The physical condition of many inner city schools is worse than deplorable. What is truly inexcusable is the shortage (and sometimes lack) of books, libraries, films, musical instruments, and other supportive, technical services. Having said that, the fact remains that if we built new schools and changed nothing else, educational outcomes would not discernibly improve. As long as we do not take seriously "what children are and where they are," new buildings are just that: new buildings.

2. It is understandable if the parents of these children want more than a token role in matters educational. I accept fully the political principle that those who will be affected by a decision or policy should have participated in the formulation of it. Let us (Blacks, Hispanics, *and* whites), however, not gloss over the fact that where this political principle has been implemented the desired outcomes have rarely been achieved. I know I sound like a broken record, but the political principle is no substitute for the educational principle contained in the big idea.

3. The parents of minority children are justified in saying that those who teach their children should understand the social-cultural context from which they come. However, it does not follow that if their teachers come from a similar

context, they grasp and act on the big idea. On the contrary, there is evidence that they approach these children in no way different than teachers from different backgrounds. In fact, back in the late sixties or early seventies a year-long observational study of classrooms in an inner city school (in St. Louis, I think) indicated that Black teachers were "harder" on, more critical of Black children than white teachers were. (It was in a book by Professor Ray Rist.)

4. It would be lunacy in the extreme to deny that the plight of our inner city schools reflects past discrimination and immorality. It would be equally crazy to deny that, generally speaking, and despite the elimination of legal-constitutional-political barriers, whites, on the one hand, and Blacks and Hispanics, on the other hand, continue to possess very negative stereotypes of each other. What would occasion surprise is if the situation were otherwise. The most unfortunate consequence has been that many (by no means all) minority children grow up in a peer culture that disparages the traditional criteria by which educational outcomes are judged. Matters are not helped any by their experience of schooling as boring, dull, and a form of harassment. We do not need any more studies of dropouts in inner city schools to tell us that far too many minority children regard schooling as a form of child abuse.

5. This is important: Whatever studies have been done on the attitudes of minority parents toward education shows them to place as high a value on education as any other group. They want their children to learn and succeed, to have a better life than they have had. And they *depend* on our schools to compensate for what they cannot do to support the personal, social, intellectual development of their children. They are bewildered, disillusioned, and angry when they see their dreams go up in smoke. They end up bitter and disillusioned, and they blame schools in particular and white society in general, thereby unwittingly contributing to more polarization.

6. These minority parents are typically American in viewing education as a form of secular salvation. And they are typically American in scapegoating schools when salvation is not on the horizon. And, crucially, they are typically

American in their imprisonment in a conception of how a school should be organized, the role of "pouring in" teacher, the role of the "dutiful," obedient student, and the necessity of a predetermined, graded curriculum. It is a conception that implicitly (and in practice explicitly) has no place for the big idea.

7. There are limits to what schools can accomplish *even if they were to take the big idea seriously*. You have put education at the top of the national agenda but you know well—as you have clearly said in your speeches—that unless we put flesh on the bones of *hope* we cannot expect minority children to see education as instrumental to a future for which they should strive. That is, to me, as obviously valid as the big idea.

Let us face it: Education has become embroiled in conflicts about race, politics, economics, power struggles, population changes, competitiveness with other countries, and a lot more. One would have hoped that out of all of this turmoil there would have come challenges to our accustomed conceptions of the factors that make for productive learning. But, no, neither from whites, nor Blacks, nor Hispanics, nor any other group, have come challenges to what schools are or have been. In regard to education we have been tinkerers. Over the last few decades there have been calls for "radical reform"—not only calls but money—but these calls have, generally speaking, led us nowhere. No one has taken seriously that the word and concept education derives from the Latin "educo": to get out, to bring out what is inside. *Wrapped up in that Latin verb is the big idea.* Not a pouring in, not a foisting upon, not an ignoring of what is *in and going on in* the minds and lives of learners.

In the past decade there has been a raging controversy about multicultural education. There is a real kernel of truth to the idea that children should be acquainted with their cultural-racial roots, present and past. But "should be" does not mean they *are*. And "should be" becomes self-defeating when it leads to a predetermined, adult-relevant curriculum which is *poured into* students.

My parents made sure I went to Hebrew School on Sundays to learn about Judaism. There was a curriculum, and we were seen as empty vessels waiting to be filled. Our teachers were heroically committed to the task of making us "good Jews" who knew and understood our heritage. They failed, not only with me but with all my friends. They never entered our Jewish world, they never sought to determine what questions we had about Judaic history, ritual, the Bible, and God. What we *had* to learn was arid, unusable, uninteresting, and eminently forgettable. Today I know I needed what they wanted me to learn and understand, and there is a part of me that is angry that they went about it in a way guaranteed to extinguish interest and curiosity. I am the poorer for it. My teachers were not villains, they were victims of a conception of "what and where children are" that turned us off, not on.

Frankly, I think I should not have tried to answer your question in the confines of a letter because the answer is a good example of "everything is related to everything else." That is the case here. If I had to put my hedgehog answer in the form of a recommendation it would be like so: Beware of any proposal from *any* group that does not explicitly accept the big idea—or, if it does, make sure it draws the appropriate conclusion about what life in a classroom should be. Such a policy or proposal would be truly radical, so contrary to what is as to arouse controversy. And it is at that point, Mr. President, that your moral leadership becomes absolutely crucial.

Respectfully,

Seymour B. Sarason

P.S. I'll take up in my next letter your acute observation that I talk mainly about young children. You will then become more aware of my limitations in knowledge and experience at the same time that the circumference of my hedgehog mind will appear a mite larger than it has.

XI

Dear Mr. and Mrs. President:

Esther said something the other day which she has said many times before, with which I agree, but which we have been reluctant to say out loud. On a couple of occasions when we did, we were viewed as flaky. I owe it to you and to me (us) to say it now. Dropping out of high school—I need not give you statistics—has always been considered a "negative symptom," a reflection of maladaptive features of an individual. There is another way of looking at it which leads to the conclusion that dropping out is a *realistic* response to a high school culture that many students experience as deadly boring, unrelated to their non-school contexts, and that will lead nowhere. As I shall expand on in my next letter, I have spent far more time in elementary school than in middle or high schools. But I have spent enough time in the latter, and I continue to try to read what researchers and observers say about high schools, to allow me to conclude that to regard dropping out as due to personal inadequacies is truly to blame the victim. If that is not always true, it is true far too often.

Think of it in terms of demand and supply. If schools do not supply, in some significant way, what students demand, why should they "buy" schooling? Why buy something that bears no relation to your perceived need to feel worthy, competent, productive, and the sense of belonging? Why buy something that far from giving you "kicks" puts you to sleep? At the very least, should we not say out loud that from the supply-demand criterion high schools in particular have had and will continue to have a shrinking market? Or, as in the case of the Detroit car makers who required decades to confront the fact that they were not competitive, will we continue to tinker, to "strengthen" what we have been doing even though it has not been effective, sedulously to avoid the question: On the basis of past experience, on the basis of scads of research, on the basis of what we know about the ingredients of productive learning and its contexts, *would we, if we had the opportunity to start from scratch, come up with high schools similar to what we have*? I have *never* spoken to a teacher or administrator who replied in the affirmative. They, no less than their students, don't buy high schools as they are. There is nothing inherently wrong with mass production, except when the number of faulty products do not pass muster.

Respectfully,

Seymour B. Sarason

P.S. I hope my letters are not depressing you. But I have no alternative to speaking the truth to power. If, as I clearly hope, you are developing a realistic picture of what you as President will be up against if you take the big idea seriously, I do not envy you. The punch line of my favorite Jewish joke is: "It could be worse, I could be in your position." But I do envy you the opportunity to initiate policies and actions that insure that you will be more than a footnote in future history books.

XII

Dear Mr. President:

I am not used to getting a personal letter from the President containing two very short, handwritten questions. (White House stationery is impressive *and* intimidating.) "What are your thoughts on a federally administered national assessment of school achievement? Should there be a national curriculum?" I know, as you do, that a civil war about these issues has been raging in educational circles for at least the last fifteen years. After my next letter I'll respond to your questions. Let me first say here that the policies suggested by these questions are examples of doing what we know we can do, *not* what needs to be done. I am reminded of the joke about the man who in the dead of winter felt ill and went to the doctor who after examining him said: "Go home, take off all your clothes, open up all the windows, stand in front of them, and breathe deeply." The patient was aghast. "But, doctor, if I do that I'll get pneumonia." To which the doctor replied, "*That* I know how to treat." Enough said.

Respectfully,

Seymour B. Sarason

P.S. Please don't conclude from the above that I regard the questions as without merit. They talk to secondary, not primary issues.

XIII

Dear Mr. and Mrs. President:

You were right in intuiting that the bulk of my direct experience has been in elementary schools. I didn't "plan" it that way. It is certainly the case that my involvement derived from my interest in prevention, i.e., what opportunities existed in *any* school for the prevention of problems? I quickly had to confront the facts of the size and organization of schools. More specifically, in comparison to elementary schools, middle and high schools are obviously and dramatically larger, both in terms of physical size and population density. In addition, and perhaps more crucially, they are organized in ways that make it extraordinarily difficult for teachers to get to know students and vice versa. You know that lovely song the teacher sings to the Emperor's children in *The King and I*: "Getting to Know You." Middle and high schools make a mockery of the message in that song, which, I must point out *again*, expresses the big idea. Rhetoric aside, teachers do not feel they know their students and students feel no one knows them (which is one reason why these schools have assistant principals, guidance counselors, and other supportive-clinical services). Adding insult to injury, it is also the case that teachers know each other in superficial ways. It is one thing to say that these schools are departmentalized—which sounds awfully "grown-up" and efficient— it is quite another thing to imply that it is an administrative structure serving the goals of productive education. It is a structure (interacting with size) conducive to anonymity, impersonal relationships, and the opposite of a sense of belonging. Whatever we have learned about productive contexts for learning and growth—*not only for students but for teachers as well*—do not exist in middle and high schools, the usual exceptions aside (about which I will write in some future letter).

I'll never forget the time I tried to arrange a meeting with five high school teachers during the school day. It was literally impossible. I wanted to meet during the day because I had already learned that by the end of the school day teachers were drained and not exactly enthusiastic about discussing and thinking through problems. The point of this anecdote is not that I could not meet with them but that there was no way or time in the school day for these teachers to meet *with each other*. It was as if the structure were locked in concrete. It existed and everyone had to adjust to it. Fairness requires that I say that teachers in these schools never denied that "getting to know" students was somewhat short of impossible. If a teacher has Johnny in a fifty-minute class once a day, and that teacher has five or six such classes, how can he or she get to know Johnny? As one teacher said to me, "It takes me at least a month to match names with faces, except for students who are unusually bright or disturbed." Bonds between teacher and student, and collegiality among teachers, are virtually nonexistent.

What I am describing is obvious. Teachers and students (and parents) know it. It has long been known that for students (i.e., many of them) the transition from elementary to middle and from middle to high school is problem producing. Too many feel and are "lost." Once more: If you believe that schools should be based, among other things, on "what and where children are," a process of getting to know them and their worlds, then our middle and high schools are screamingly counterproductive.

What I observed in these schools was the manufacture of problems. Prevent problems? Forget it, and I did. I ended up feeling more alone and discouraged than ever. But I did not conclude that this situation was the fault of educators, as if they colluded to produce the self-defeating condition. Teachers and administrators have been prepared, trained, to accept and to adjust to the size and structure of these schools. They are no less unwitting victims in this regard than are their students. How all this came about is a long, long story that has been told by many historians of education. But who reads the historians? To understand all is not to forgive all. There is plenty of blame to go around, e.g., some educational theorists, our unimaginative, self-serving schools of education, the lack of bold educational and political leadership, and a business-industrial community that *viewed* students, if at all, as they did raw material: something to be molded and shaped in as cheap and efficient a way as possible. I italicized "viewed" because leaders in the private sector *now* know that something is radically wrong, that the United States is becoming a "dropout." Unfortunately, they have no inkling of the big idea or its implications.

Esther says I should refrain from using my corny jokes, which she has heard for almost sixty years, so I hardly blame her. But it is a very short joke which contains a principle I want to state. Papa says to Izzy, "Close the door it is cold outside." Izzy's response is, "So if I close the door it will still be cold outside." The equivalent of the father's demand of Izzy is that we downsize these schools so that they are more "humane," i.e., they permit and sustain those kinds and qualities of relationships (for teachers and students) so essential to the desire to learn. The equivalent to Izzy's response is that if that change came about, and that is all you do, and that change is not powered by the big idea, the educational experience will not have changed. I may be too pessimistic about this. Independent of anything else I would enthusiastically endorse any effort to downsize these schools as a step to making "getting to know you" a possibility. But hedgehog me has to say that unless this downsizing is in the most explicit way for the purpose of taking seriously "what and where students are," educational outcomes will not markedly improve—which brings me to my experience in elementary schools.

Elementary schools are far more "humane" than middle and high schools, if by humane you imply that the individual child stands a chance of being recognized and understood. Teachers in middle and high schools are oriented to their particular subject matters. I am sure, Mrs. President, that in your preparation as a teacher you were told that you teach children, not subject matter. Teachers in middle and high schools (like college teachers) teach subject matter, i.e., they start where they, the teachers, are, not where students are; they "pour in" the predetermined curriculum, they are not set to "draw or get out" what is in the minds of students. On the level of rhetoric, at least, elementary school teachers say they are quite aware of the adverse consequences of teaching subject matter, not children. And it is true, in my experience, that elementary school teachers are more interested in their pupils as people than are middle and high school teachers. Having said this, I have to go on to say that elementary school teachers, no less than other teachers, have little or no grasp of the big idea. And for several reasons: They are *given* a curriculum they *must* follow, and *they* will be judged by the test scores of their students. The third reason is to me crucial: their preparation for teaching "socializes" them to view the curriculum as all important, and why and *how* to adapt it to "what and where children are" are conspicuously absent in almost all of these programs. This explains the "page 31 syndrome": by October 2, we must be up to page 31 in the curriculum! It's like the movie *If It's Tuesday, It Must Be Belgium*. You will never understand high school dropout rates, low motivation and interest, allergies to the life of the mind, the absence of a *willing* acquisition and pursuit of knowledge, and a mammoth disinterest in history and our society, unless you see their origins in elementary school. It is in elementary school where you can "hook" children, where you stand a chance to prevent, to a degree at least, derogatory attitudes to learning. Children start elementary school willingly and enthusiastically set to buy the big idea: to use the adult world to understand *their* world of questions and strivings. Yes, these young children live in a world of wonder, there is so much they want to know and understand, they want to experience "growing up," being competent, feeling worthy and alive. Reengendering that world of wonder in middle and high school students is in principle possible, but only by those whose depths of masochism are bottomless. I am not being defeatist and I am not in any way suggesting that we should give up on efforts to downsize and change middle and high schools. I am not an advocate for malign neglect. I am an advocate for taking the obvious seriously. Someone once said that my only claim to fame is that I belabored the obvious. Someone else called hedgehog me the Johnny-One-Note Professor of Psychology. Someone else called me a male Cassandra. Esther has called me other things, but at least she loves me.

Am I right in saying that several questions have occurred to you? For example:

1. How do you go about downsizing middle and high schools? Would not that require semi-astronomical expenditures?

2. How do you implement the big idea without causing anarchy, sacrificing accountability, and lowering standards?

3. How can we influence preparatory programs for educators so that they grasp the big idea and its implications for what goes on in the classroom?

4. How do you "sell" all of this to the American people who are not likely to take the long-term view?

As I said in an earlier letter, I do not want to be perceived as all-knowing, as a deviser of blueprints that tell you how to "build," as an engineer of institutional-societal change. I think I know my strengths, which is to say I know my limits. I don't like the way this will sound but I have to say it: Everything in my personal and professional experience absolutely confirms the moral and developmental validity of the big idea, and the failure to take that idea seriously has consigned most people—white, Black, rich, poor—to what they come to see as an empty, purpose-seeking existence in which the sparks of creativity have been extinguished. I don't state that indictment lightly. And, as I have emphasized, I am by no means the first either to articulate the big idea or to see what the absence of that idea has wrought.

There are those who will describe me as a semi-senile, isolated, deservedly retired professor who is incapable of seeing that the world has changed, and who writes as if all children should or are capable of going to Yale (or Harvard if Yale rejects them). I, they will go on to say, do not live in the real world and that what I expect of children is wildly utopian. To which I reply, "Balderdash!" (truly a weak word). These are criticisms from people who in the entire post World War II era have been wrong about our schools, who have bought damned near every nostrum for improving schools, and some of whom committed the most egregious of all (a typically American error): They assumed that spending money guaranteed improvement. How more unrealistic can you get?

Forgive me for exploding. It's not that I am defending myself—I'm way past that except, of course, with Esther. Rather it was a response to the possibility that the two of you may find what I say about the big idea as too abstract or general and providing no guidelines for action. So, what I am going to do in my next letter is to tell you about three studies that I, and everyone who has ever read them, found monumentally inspiring. If that letter is not convincing, then I see no point in continuing our conversation. That is a promise, not a threat. And, needless to say, if that letter is not convincing I shall attribute it to my inadequacies as a writer, inadequacies, I have been assured many times, I have more than a few. It will not change my belief in the big idea at all. After all, hedgehogs, especially of the very senior citizen species, are willing captives of their big idea.

Respectfully,

Seymour B. Sarason

P.S. I anticipate difficulty with that next letter because I will have to summarize three books: two by a well-known poet, and one by an art educator, theorist, and historian who was the greatest intellectual influence in my adult years. Fear not, there will be no quotations, jargon, or the abstract musings of an academic. What you will get is description, concluding, of course, with a brief (I promise) sermon. It may take me a couple of weeks. Mr. President, with all that confronts you in the oval office, you can use a vacation from the likes of me.

XIV

Dear Mrs. President:

I can't say it any other way: It was sweet of you to write that reassuring letter. I anticipated that you would have no difficulty grasping the big idea because you were a teacher who, as you say, "from day one experienced a battle between the demands of *the* curriculum and what I would have done if I were *free*." I like the way you italicize! I accept (with relief and gratitude) your statement that your husband grasps the significance of the big idea at the same time that both of you are not sure what that means for policy and action. I'm not all that sure either. That is not a confession but, I think and hope, realistic modesty. You are kind, probably too kind, in your assessment of me and what I have written over the years. Since these are confidential letters, may I tell you how I assess myself? In the land of the blind, the *one-eyed*, *astigmatic* man is king! Of the appropriateness of the italicized words, I am certain.

Respectfully,

Seymour B. Sarason

P.S. Your letter caused Esther to say, "Thank God the President's wife is one of the fortunate few who learns from and can change because of experience." Esther is one of the fortunate few who in her career as a psychotherapist managed to *unlearn* much of what she was taught. Needless to say, she was most appreciative of your warm words about her continuing supervision of someone who in matters of health has learned little from experience.

XV

Dear Mr. and Mrs. President:

I begin with Henry Schaefer-Simmern, a political refugee from Hitler's Germany. Of all the hedgehogs I have known, he takes the cake. His big idea—and he was by no means the first to articulate it—had three parts:

1. Every human being is born with the potential to be creative and artistic.

2. Wherever on this earth *very* young children are observed and studied, they engage in and get delight from artistic activity that contains all the seeds of what we conventionally call art or artistic activity.

3. Those seeds get extinguished for a variety of reasons, not the least of which is the belief that *visual* artistic activity and its products should conform to or represent what is "real." In erecting that conformity as *the* criterion we virtually guarantee that children will come to see themselves as unartistic. That is most clear in what passes for art education in our schools.

So what did Schaefer do? Before he came to the United States he had worked with scores of groups of "ordinary" people, workers most of whom were of the blue-collar variety. And "working with" meant providing the opportunity to engage in and develop their potential for visual-artistic expression. The most difficult obstacle he predictably encountered was the attitude, "Who am I to try to be an artist?" But Schaefer being Schaefer—a tall, imposing, passionate, hedgehog—attracted "students."

Schaefer *never* told a person what or how to draw. He started with a suggestion: "Draw what you want to see so that you see it the way you want to see it, however simple it may be." Following which he would ask the person, "Do you like what you have done? Study it. Is there anything you

want to change? Is there something in your picture that
bothers you, that is not clear? Do you want to try again?"
The long and short of it is that Schaefer received much
acclaim in Europe from the exhibits of the works of his
students. Paintings, rugs, sculpture were some of the media
students employed. I and many other people have seen
photos of these works. Do they deserve to be in museums?
That question would throw Schaefer into a rage, assuming
as that question did that artistic activity did not have value
in itself and for the individual. As he liked to put it, "When
we form something through artistic activity, we are formed
and changed in the process, and that spurs the developmental process." I have never known anyone who saw those
photos who would not have loved to have the originals on
the walls of their homes.

Before telling you about Schaefer and me I have to say
something about language. However good language is as a
form of communication, it is very inadequate for describing
visual works of art. It is one thing to describe a work of art,
it is quite another to see it. Therefore, I have asked the
University of California Press at Berkeley to send you a copy
of *The Unfolding of Artistic Activity*, which was published
over fifty years ago. What I will now tell you will be compellingly conveyed in that book. Incidentally, one of our
greatest psychologists, philosophers, and educators—John
Dewey, of course—wrote the introduction to that book.
There are times when greatness recognizes greatness.

I met Schaefer in 1942 at the Southbury Training School,
a residential state institution for mentally defective individuals. (Today we say mentally retarded but in those days it
was mentally defective.) He wanted, he said, to demonstrate
that *even* mentally defective individuals had the potential to
develop artistically. He showed me the photos of the work
of "ordinary" people in Germany.

He had secured a Russell Sage Foundation fellowship to
demonstrate his ideas with those who had even less of life's
advantages. When I saw the photos, wise-guy me immediately concluded, first, they were not works of ordinary people and, second, it was fantasy to believe that Schaefer had
not told his students what to draw and how to proceed. That

"our" children—regardless of age they were all considered children, and my guess is the average age of the population was in the twenties—had potential for artistic development was patently ridiculous. But Russell Sage had arranged with our superintendent for Schaefer to have a studio at Southbury. I was to help him select "students," to be as helpful as possible, and to observe what went on. I did not look kindly at our superintendent or at the prospect of interacting with someone who knew zilch about mental deficiency.

That I was wrong is the understatement of the century, if not in recorded history. These "children" were not supposed to be capable of working willingly and enthusiastically for more than a very short time, but what I saw were people struggling for as much as three hours at a stretch to give form to their internal imagery. And, wonder of wonders, *they* decided what they wanted to do. Schaefer's role was to study with each of them *each* of their products. Where or when did they have trouble? Could they "fix" it if they tried again? Maybe they should use a larger piece of paper or different colors? Together they studied the product as if it was the most important thing on earth. Schaefer never suggested content. He started where *they* were, what *they* were trying to express in organized form. He organized an exhibit of their work and the employees came in droves, were amazed at the same time that they were suspicious about who the "real" artist was.

So when you see his book—which includes his work with low IQ, institutionalized juvenile delinquents and with "ordinary" Americans who had never engaged in artistic activity—

you will see concretely the validity of his big idea as well as the big idea I have been talking about: You start with what is in the heads of children. Incidentally, in 1992 Ray Berta of St. Mary's College in California completed a dissertation in Stanford's School of Education on Schaefer: his work, pedagogy, and his challenge to our schools in general and to art education in particular. That dissertation is a work of art about an art educator and theorist who has never received the recognition he deserves. Not so incidentally, some of the most distinguished people of this century in art and the humanities recognized, as Berta documents, Schaefer's achievements. The art-educational establishment did not and has not. Please send me your reactions to his book. If it has the same dust jacket it used to have, you will see a great work of art by a social worker whose first, faltering efforts were stick figures. Schaefer traces her development step-by-step. But he did that for every student. The data, the raw data, the evidence are all in the book. Enjoy.

Now I have to ask you to use your imagination. Imagine a run-of-the-mill nursing home on New York's lower east side. And when I say run-of-the-mill I mean a place where its very aged residents are waiting for death. People sit around, many in wheelchairs, dozing or sleeping, the TV is on but few are watching, all in a day or recreational (what a euphemism!) room where no one talks to anyone else. (I know whereof I talk. My father was in a "good" nursing home for two years. With goodness like that, badness will never be in short supply.)

Enter Kenneth Koch, a very well-known poet from Columbia University. And what does this well-intentioned, obviously misguided professor want to do? He wants the residents to write poetry, *their* poetry. How he proceeded and with what rationale, the attitudinal obstacles in the residents he had to overcome, what happened when the sparks of creative activity became a fire, how these "not with it" people became with it and artistically productive—it is all in his book (plus, of course, their poetry): *I Never Told Anybody*. Since I no longer am able to go to the university, I do not know (remember) who the publisher was or if the book is still in print. But you do have the Congressional Library at your disposal!

What Professor Koch demonstrated with nursing home residents he also demonstrated with Black and Hispanic elementary school children in a ghetto school. It is all in his inspiring, delightful, tradition shattering book *Wishes, Lies, and Dreams*. I am wrong; it should have been tradition-shattering but like many books that get critical acclaim, it had, for all practical purposes, no general impact.

Sermon

There is evil in this world. So what else is new? Evil is easy to identify and to fight. Far more subtle and consequential is the tendency to underestimate what people are and can be. You can write human history as a series of battles against that tendency. It is not a malevolently motivated tendency but rather one about opposing visions of the human animal who is essentially a social one. And the opposing forces know full well that if what is considered "right, natural, and proper"—what philosophers call the accepted world view—is altered, the institutions that are undergirded by that view will be, will have to be, dramatically different than they have been. That is why the big idea is resisted: valued in rhetoric but denied in practice. Once you take that idea seriously, you can never look at schools in the usual way.

Sylvia Ashton Warner's book is *not* about learning to read, period. Schaefer-Simmern's book is *not* about artistic activity, period. Kenneth Koch's books are *not* about poetry, period. What these books are about is how one recognizes, capitalizes on, and nurtures the universal need to give *formed* expression—mindless expressiveness is an abomination—to one's imagery, ideas, questions, and feelings. Not somebody else's but one's own. We are *questing* organisms: asking, searching, pondering, experimenting, puzzling about ourselves and our worlds. And this from our earliest days. We do not deny or reject the worlds of others but we seek to understand them in terms of our world. But when those other worlds deny or reject or are disinterested in our world—I am describing schools, of course, and more—we retreat and erect unbridgeable walls between those worlds. Schools, nursing homes, and institutions for mentally retarded people are very different kinds of physical places, but they are identical in that they are based on and suffer from the dynamics of the self-fulfilling prophecy: They start with a conception of what people are and can be and end up proving it with the best of intentions. Those responsible for these places are not villains, they are bright, dedicated, hard-working people. They are imprisoned in conceptions that do not permit them to see how self-defeating those conceptions are.

Warner, Schaefer-Simmern, and Koch worked with wildly different populations and used different media. But they had one pedagogical principle without which their achievements are inexplicable. It is a principle each of them articulates in plain, unvarnished English: *You start with where your students are,* not with what you want them to think and learn, and always with the ultimate goal of bridging different worlds.

Not long after the Russian Revolution, Lincoln Steffens visited the Soviet Union and when he returned proclaimed, "I have seen the future and it works." For the past thirty-five years I have been saying about schools: "I have seen the future and, like the past, it doesn't work." In no way am I drawing an analogy between Stalinist tyranny and slaughters, on the one hand, and what happens to children in our schools. Stalin knew exactly what he was doing and why; he had no peer in the castle of history's villains. Stalin was evil incarnate. As I said before, in regard to education there are no villains, no one willed the present situation. That is why the situation is so worrisome and why changing it will be so difficult. I do not envy you.

Respectfully,

Seymour B. Sarason

P.S. If it is the case that the truth shall set you free, it is also the case that the truth can make you feel awfully alone.

P.S. One more time: What I have said in my letters has been said by others in the near and distant past. If, as is the case, I do not have the corner on the truth, I, at least, respect history. My fate has been to be witness to what others far more wise than I have said.

P.S. I find it strange that, although at this moment I feel drained, I also feel exhilarated. Indeed, we are strange animals!

XVI

Dear Mrs. Third Lady:

My cup runneth over! I not only receive a letter from you but also one from the President who, in what I assume to be a characteristic way, is brief and direct. (His handwriting is legible, at least more so than that of my physicians for my prescriptions.) "Please outline for me two or three very specific suggestions for programs I should send to Congress. Listen to your wife and stay healthy."

Yes, I know the pressure your husband is feeling. He is betwixt and between, and so am I. On the one hand, I want to be specific and, on the other hand, the more specific I get the more it may appear inadequate as a response to that overwhelming feeling—as plaguing as it is understandable— that things are going from bad to worse and we have to move on all fronts *now*. And by fronts is meant *new* fronts, and there is the rub! What and where are the new fronts? I'll do my best.

Respectfully,

Seymour B. Sarason

XVII

Dear Mr. and Mrs. President:

How do you take the big idea seriously? What does an elementary school teacher have to know *and* do to permit us to say that he or she is taking the idea seriously? That the teacher has to know subject matter goes without saying. That is the easy part. What is not so easy is getting teachers to believe in the big idea, a degree of belief permitting them to say, "I *know* that if I take the idea seriously, children will learn what we and they want to learn." To be able to articulate that kind of "know" requires that teachers have seen or observed what that means in practice. It is not a matter of accepting the big idea in the abstract or plunging ahead with good intentions and no experience. It is a matter of proceeding on the basis of personal experience of some kind and degree.

Take numbers, for example. How do you meld the "two worlds" in the case of numbers? What would be helpful to teachers? One thing that would be helpful would be a film in which, *starting* with day one of the school year, a person could *see* what it means to take the big idea seriously *in a real* classroom with real children. *Not* an edited film from which has been deleted problems and difficulties. Not a film which conveys the message: it's easy. It is not easy, it demands understandings, tolerance of blind alleys, and a capacity to resist returning to the "pouring in" mold. After all, it is a new way of looking at kids and yourself. It is not only a "how to do it" process but a "how to think about it" one as well. The point is that it is not enough *to talk* or *discuss* the big idea. What teachers need is literally to see what the big idea entails in the real world of classrooms. They have to see what it means developmentally, step-by-step over the life of a classroom. My task in writing to you would have been easier and briefer if I could have sent you two such films: one in a classroom based on the big idea and one from a traditional classroom in the same school.

Such films do not exist for any subject matter. The reasons are many so I will only mention a few of the major ones.

1. Those who teach teachers subject matter (math, social studies, reading, etc.) are interested primarily in subject matter *only*. They are not concerned with the big idea or any other idea about productive learning. They judge themselves, and are judged by others, by how well teachers comprehend the structure and logic of the subject matter. They are interested in and teach adults, not children. (I have known a handful of exceptions.)

2. Those who teach teachers pedagogy (methods courses) do so in terms of the traditional classroom: the teacher is in charge, the teacher instructs, the teacher is the fount of knowledge, the teacher is the executive, the legislature, and the judiciary. The big idea is unconstitutional! The teacher *has* to be in control, and the big idea is seen as an invitation to anarchy, or wastefulness of time, or sacrificing *the* curriculum, or all of the above even though *in the abstract* no educator disputes the big idea.

3. Believe it or not, the research community has shown little interest (the exceptions aside) in studying the big idea with real children in real classrooms even though, again, I have never met a researcher who disputed the big idea.

4. A researcher once said to me: "How can you dispute the big idea? But can you dispute the fact that schools and school systems would throw up their hands in horror if I asked them to allow me and their teachers to take the big idea seriously for a month, let alone a year? If I asked them, it would be the shortest conversation." I'll say more about this later.

The federal government cannot and should not force schools to change how classrooms are to be organized and what the content of curricula should be. What the federal government can do is to provide *incentives* for schools to change. And one of those incentives is to provide them with *visual* evidence of what is involved when the big idea is taken seriously. Not a written report, not books, not inspirational sermons, but sustained, compelling visual narratives, warts and all.

My concrete proposal is that the federal government invite proposals to develop films on the implementation of the big idea in real classrooms and schools over an entire year. This would require, of course, that a school willingly and explicitly gives up anything resembling adherence to the curriculum it has used in the particular grade being studied. *That, I hasten to add, does not mean there is no curriculum.* The goal always is to meld two worlds, two curricula, the worlds of the children and the adults. It would also require willingness on the part of teachers and parents. And it would require the co-equal participation of researchers not only committed to the big idea but also to the rules of evidence.

This would not be an inexpensive action research program, especially, as I would hope, if one gets proposals from a variety of schools: rich and poor, white and Black and Hispanic, urban and rural. At the very least, it would provide us with visual documentation of what is involved in taking the big idea seriously: Its problems, its potentials, and how it stands up in comparison to the modal, non-stimulating classroom. If it should turn out—I am willing to bet and give odds—that these films will be compelling if not wholly convincing, they will be an incentive for schools to change. Changing by fiat *never* has worked. Changing by incentives is our best bet.

You, certainly your educational advisors, have access to sophisticated researchers, sophisticated in regard to research methodology, evidence, and interpretation. What I am saying is that they know what "honest" action research entails. This kind of action research is not easy. Let us not forget that this is research that will be carried out in real classrooms in real schools, which means that one should not be surprised when one encounters the unexpected and the unintended. The big idea is an old one. From the standpoint of practice it is revolutionary, involving as it does changing understandings, attitudes, and actions.

I have given you an "idea" about a possible federal initiative. Believe me, I could write a book about how *not* to go about this kind of action research. (In fact, I wrote several books on the subject. Plug.) What I have suggested is no panacea. It is no more and no less than an effort to obtain that kind of visual "data" that would permit the viewer to see what life in the classroom is and could be, i.e., to go beyond rhetoric, beyond name calling, beyond arid theorizing, beyond posturing, beyond stances that view risk-taking a subversion of tradition.

Films and television changed the modern world (for good and bad). Can there be any doubt that when the histories of the twentieth century are written, there will be absolute agreement that being able literally to see the world changed peoples'— all peoples'—attitudes and expectations dramatically?

I have to tell you an unpleasant but relevant story. A young friend of mine, who is Jewish, got into an argument with a co-worker who expressed doubt about the extent and details of Hitler's attempt to exterminate European Jewry. The co-worker did not deny Hitler's animus toward Jews. He simply did not believe that what happened was as gory, as fantastically sadistic, as the picture of the Holocaust that was painted. My young friend was aghast. What he did was go to New York to get from the public and commercial television stations a list of the film footage of concentration and extermination (they were not the same) camps on the days when they were liberated by the allied forces. (The U.S. Army has thousands of feet of such films.) I had seen many of these films. If a person has a tendency to vomit, he should have a pail nearby when he or she watches the films. Michelangelo's mural of hell in the Sistine Chapel is a comedy compared to what is in these films. My young Jewish friend invited his co-worker to go with him to New York to see some of the films. The co-worker was never the same again: What he saw he could not deny or get around.

It is obvious, I hope, that I did not relate this anecdote to draw any comparison between the Holocaust and our schools. I may be old, weary, stupid, and crabby, but crazy I am not. But it is an anecdote that illustrates the obvious: What is visually compelling has an unrivalled dynamic that language *and* our fantasies frequently do not. It's one thing to talk about classrooms, it is quite another thing to see them.

Respectfully,

Seymour B. Sarason

P.S. Several years ago I had to adjust to the fact that I was no longer physically up to writing a book. Although mentally and psychologically I felt I was Bar Mitzvahed yesterday and ready to grow up, my body disagreed. I tell you this because writing to you has really started the juices flowing again. This is but a way of saying that what I have written to you are not ideas but skeletons of ideas I would love to give life to. In any event, having your ears really recharged my batteries, for which I am grateful.

P.S. What I have said about films reminded me of a similar proposal I made fifty years ago, a proposal with which everyone agreed and no one bought. I'll tell you about it in my next letter. My track record for persuasion or making a difference in this world is not impressive! There is a "lesson" in this, but I don't want to know it!

P.S. I am enjoying the fantasy that I am President and addressing Congress on my educational programs. What would the introduction to that speech be? It would be no more than four or five pages. Would you like me to write it? You don't have to answer that question. As with everything I have ever written, I take pencil to paper and then, and only then, do I find out what I have been thinking. That's why writing has always been so satisfying: I discover what has been going on in my head. Only once did I start a book, write the first chapter, and give up. It was after we did a major reconstruction and renovation of our house. The title of the book was *The Contribution of the Construction Trades to Mental Illness.* By the end of that first chapter I discovered a bottomless well of hostility my better judgment said I should not plumb.

XVIII

Dear Mr. and Mrs. President:

Professionally speaking, I grew up in the field of mental retardation. One of the first problems I encountered—a problem for which I was not in the slightest prepared—was how to convey to parents what the diagnosis of mental retardation meant for them and their child. By the time I saw the parents they had already been through the mill of being "talked to" by physicians, psychologists, educators, and others. The long and short of it was that I learned the hard way that there was *no* professional field that prepared its practitioners for how you talk with parents in an honest, sensitive, helpful way. It was not happenstance that the revolution in mental retardation that started in the fifties was largely led by parents who had their fill of professionals and their conceptions of being helpful.

When I came to Yale I began a research project that involved me in the public schools. That is when I learned that long before the cold war between the West and the then Soviet Union, there was the cold war between parents and educators. It showed up around all kinds of problems, too numerous to mention. It was hard to avoid the impression that educators defined heaven as a place where you did not have to deal with parents, or where parents respectfully went along with what educators recommended. It was impossible to avoid the impression that when parents were asked to meet with their child's teacher or principal, they came with a mixture of feelings: fear, anger, and impotence.

I got involved in a teacher preparation program in a nearby college. My major foci were (a) to get the students to begin to comprehend what was involved in having a mutually satisfactory meeting with a parent, and (b) that we were not born with genes that "told us" how to do it.

What I could do in one teacher training program had the obvious limitation: I was trying to make a difference in *one* small program. However fascinating and instructive the experience was for me and the students, it was not sufficient to satisfy my need to save and change the world. I never fooled myself about the scope of my ambition!

So I proposed to God knows how many people and organizations that I (or somebody else) develop films on talking with parents about this or that issue involving their children. Not (necessarily) scripted films but ones with real parents, real problems. Not films in which professionals make no mistakes, are always composed and never falter, and inevitably and skillfully get a parent to see the light. You get the point. In addition, however, I proposed a series of films of would-be teachers—special and regular classroom teachers—to be used only by them and their supervisors for purposes of self-study.

No one ever bought my proposals. I gave up. I surfaced my proposals again during the sixties and seventies when open conflict between educators and parents erupted, especially in our cities. Those were the days when the word "communicate" became the most overworked word in the English language. You could argue, as I sometimes did, that parents and educators were "communicating" perfectly: Either they left no doubt about how little they thought of each other, or there was unverbalized agreement that talking to each other was a charade. In any event, those were years when it did not require someone like me to convince educators that having to talk to and work with parents was undeserved punishment. Wouldn't you have expected that preparatory programs for educators would have done *something*? They did *nothing*.

Films are no panacea. But the kinds of films I am talking about have at least the virtue of saying: "There is a problem. We can no longer duck it. Its ramifications are wide and deep. We have *talked* about the problem but rarely publicly and candidly. With these films, we and parents know that we have had a common experience. We may react to the films differently but at least we have a clearer, more concrete basis for understanding our differences." Yes, Mr. President, I do assume that to the extent that increasing numbers of people can *see* a problem—that in doing so it evokes their relevant experience and provokes them to thought—that problem will undergo change and gain even greater clarity. That it may stir controversy is part of the game. I am assuming, of course, that it would not take long to learn how to make films that are honest (true to their purposes), compelling, and reflective of the complexity of the issues on the level of thought and action. And that brings me to one of your and my favorite presidents: Franklin D. Roosevelt. (Hedgehog me, I've been searching for "something" that is of interest to *you* and, therefore, something I can capitalize on to engender your interest in the kinds of films I am trying to describe. Eureka, I found it, I think!)

Did you know that FDR had a "movie maker"? His name was Pare Lorentz, and in the history of films he is regarded as the father of documentaries. That FDR made him his movie maker came about in the usual strange, unpredictable ways. What cemented their relationship were several shared, overarching interests: to *preserve* the environment, to *prevent* the tragic consequences of "dust bowls" and flooding rivers, and to *educate* the public about what was at stake and what needed to be done. Today our TV screens present us with more documentaries than we have days in the year. In the thirties it was another story. Two of Lorentz's films—*The River* and *The Plow That Broke the Plains*—had a dramatic impact on public officialdom as well as the public generally. Lorentz wrote the scripts, chose the composers who wrote the music (e.g., Virgil Thompson), and did the filming. He was the right man at the right time with the right support, i.e., FDR. It was one thing for people to read about the "dust bowl" and flooding rivers, it was another thing to *see* how and why those disasters occurred. It was not an exaggeration to say that those films played an important role in the development of programs to prevent reoccurrences of what were human and environmental disasters. FDR was truly an "environmental president" and he did not need to be convinced that Pare Lorentz was a "natural resource." Together they made history. When people think about the dust bowl of the thirties, they are likely to recall John Steinbeck's *The Grapes of Wrath*, published in 1939, and, of course, the film made from the book. What people do not know is that Pare Lorentz's films antedated Steinbeck's book and had influenced him. Steinbeck and Lorentz became friends. When Lorentz died in 1992, all of his works and correspondence were placed in the Roosevelt Library in Hyde Park.

Back to education. In the past half century the federal government (via its three branches) has mightily sought to change schools, e.g., to desegregate them, to "mainstream" handicapped children, to give poor children a "head start," to fund enrichment of programs for inner city schools, and much more. All of this was done with one overarching goal: to stimulate and sustain the willing, productive pursuit of learning. Implicitly, it was a goal to prevent the incidence of school learning problems. Let me put it this way: The aim was to change what goes on in classrooms, even though there is no way that the federal government *can and should* dictate what should go on in a classroom. These programs were based on the hope that what is initiated in Washington would in some way have the intended consequences in classrooms. They did not, generally speaking. The reasons are many but certainly one of them is failure to use films as a means for depicting what classrooms are and can be. I and others—believe me, there have been others—can talk and write endlessly about what classrooms are and should be, about what the big idea means, about productive learning, but we are using language as a way to engender what we hope is appropriate imagery. Whatever the power of language in this regard, it lacks the concreteness and compellingness of *seeing*. I am reminded of the time that Esther and I were in Athens and went up to see the Parthenon. We had read about it, saw pictures of it, but when we actually *saw*, it was one of the most moving experiences of our lives.

One more thing. It has probably been a long time since you have read *The Grapes of Wrath* or seen the film, which was also superb. May I suggest that you read the book and see the film again and *then* arrange to see Lorentz's documentaries. I think that both of you will agree that his films have that "something," that perspective, which the novel and the movie do not capture: the incalculable superiority of prevention over repair, that indeed we have met the enemy and it is us.

My fantasy is that you, Mr. President, like FDR, can initiate a program from which a Pare Lorentz will emerge, a man or woman who will show us what life in a classroom is and could be. In serendipitous ways FDR and Lorentz found each other. I wish you are as lucky as FDR.

Respectfully,

Seymour B. Sarason

P.S. Re FDR and his era. I find it appalling how few people today do not know—worse yet, are uninterested in knowing—how *their* world is not understandable without knowing what happened during and because of his presidency. *Please* don't conclude that I am suggesting that we "improve" the teaching of American history. That would be the kiss of death: enlarging the museum of dates, personalities, and legislation. Why is FDR so important to *you* who, unlike me, did not live through that era? When you answer *that* question, you are on the way to understanding the role of the big idea.

P.S. Esther just reminded me of the obvious: You grew up where memories of the dust bowl and flooding rivers were more than "history." Right?

P.S. No more about films. In my next letter I will write about a second "idea" for a legislative initiative. It is more complex, difficult, and controversial than the first one because it deals with two questions: How *are* educators prepared for life in schools and classrooms, and how *should* they be prepared? With questions like that you never have to worry about a dull life.

P.S. Passover begins tomorrow night. As you may know, the celebration begins with a young child asking *the* four questions, each of which is based on Santayana's maxim that those who do not know *their* history are doomed to repeat it. Questions, questions, questions, the royal road to self-knowledge and identity! How more obvious can you get? Who takes the obvious seriously?

XIX

Dear Mr. President:

I treasure your letter less because it came from you, although that would be satisfaction enough, than because you confirmed two predictions: You got pitifully little about the FDR era in your prep school *and* in college, but you were mammothly influenced-instructed by your grandfather who lived through it all and who, unlike Steinbeck's Joad family, managed to survive and stay put. What I found absolutely fascinating in what you related was your grandfather's most frequent opening gambit: "What would *you* like me to tell you about *me*." That is a twist on the big idea that never occurred to me, even though I long ago knew that children in a classroom were as curious as hell about their teacher's life and background. To articulate that curiosity is, unfortunately, off limits, i.e., it is not part of the curriculum!

Please give my thanks to the Third Lady for supporting what I said about films. With a constituent like her, I feel empowered.

Respectfully,

Seymour B. Sarason

P.S. Re my second "idea." I'm having trouble because I wrote a book about it, and it is proving difficult to be commendably/necessarily brief. I would never have been in the running for the endowed chair of Succinct Professor of Psychology. Sounds oxymoronic! But you will get the letter within the next week or so.

P.S. I'm delighted that you "urge" me to write some prefatory remarks to your educational message to Congress. Your letter stirred up a storm of Walter Mitty fantasies I thought were extinguished in me! I'll send you my Pericles-level statement after the next (troublesome) letter.

P.S. A couple of weeks ago a former student of mine, who knows I like and collect jokes, called and told me the one about the boy who told his immigrant mother that his teacher wanted to see her. The mother went to the school where she was told by the teacher in a most serious tone, "Yesterday I asked your son who wrote *Hamlet*? He answered that he did not write Hamlet." To which the mother replied authoritatively, "If *my* son said he didn't write Hamlet, he didn't write Hamlet." So much for "communication."

XX

Dear Mr. President:

Let me start with some observations:

1. By far the bulk of past federal initiatives have been efforts at repair. Primary prevention has been distinguished by its absence, largely because it requires a long-term perspective and commitment that are not "politically sexy."

2. Preparatory programs for educators (teachers and administrators) have minimally changed over the decades. What changes have been made have been in the form of cosmetic add-ons. They have and continue to prepare educators for schools as they are, not what they should or might be.

3. Beginning in the sixties four issues became public and controversial: the allocation of power and responsibility among school personnel, alternative rationales for classroom organization and management, school-community relationships, and the nature and aims of a standardized curriculum. Preparatory programs hardly deal with these issues, which is to say that when educators go out into the real world of schools, they are conceptually and politically virginal to a degree that is disillusioning and upsetting to *them*.

4. The big idea is in no way a set of principles informing or determining "the curriculum" of preparatory programs.

5. All of the above (and more) explains why there is a very large consulting industry, the aim of which is to repair or change how educators think and act. Just as in medicine most physicians devote their time to repair, the same is true for the educational consulting industry as well as for many federally supported programs. Just as departments of public health— where prevention is taken seriously—are second class citizens in medical schools, that is the fate of those who

take primary prevention seriously in education. The healer has far more status (and funding) than the preventer!

What deserves emphasis, Mr. President, is that the inadequacies of preparatory programs produce problems both for students *and* educators. It is myopic in the extreme to be concerned only for the educational development of children. What happens to educators in their careers is of co-equal importance with what happens to students in their careers in school.

So what do we do? You start, of course, with a question: What would a preparatory program for educators look like if it took primary prevention seriously? For hedgehog me I start with this question: What would a program look like if it was organized around the big idea? Put in this way, how would you "educate" educators to experience, to understand, to be comfortable with, to implement the big idea in classrooms?

(My swan song book on education was on this issue, and that is why I am having trouble with this letter. It is far more complicated than I can indicate here. It's not unlike what Winston Churchill said about the then Soviet Union: a puzzle wrapped up in mystery at the core of which is an enigma. I found an extra copy of the book, which I am sending to the Third Lady. If she, having been through a preparatory program, does not hear the ring of truth when she reads the book, I will be surprised. I know she has a mind of her own, for which you should thank God for very big favors.)

This is crucial: *No preparatory program committed to the big idea should proceed unless it obtains a similar commitment from one or more school systems.* The reason is obvious: classrooms and curricula will be dramatically different than they now are, and that is something cooperating school systems have to understand. However simple the big idea is, its consequences for action are enormous and to gloss over that fact is to guarantee failure. At the present time preparatory programs "give" schools what they say they want, even though what they want is part of the problem.

A concrete proposal: The federal government should make funds available to preparatory programs and cooperating school systems explicitly committed to engage in an educational revolution. I do not use the word revolution cavalierly. I use it in precisely the same way as our founding fathers did when they began their Declaration of Independence with the words "When in the course of human affairs . . ."—their justification for starting the revolution. Similarly, when in the course of our national affairs our educational system no longer is serving national interests, we should not, must not, shirk from revolutionary ideas and actions.

I deliberately left one thing out in my proposal and I did so in order to make a point. What I left out is that state departments of education would also have to commit themselves to the new programs, meaning that they are willing to eschew or relax *any* requirement that would violate the spirit of the new programs. The point is, Mr. President, that there are many vested interests in the educational arena. As a sophisticated and obviously successful politician, you need no lesson about complicated, interrelated, symbiotic vested interests. How you work with them, or get around them, or run over them, or all of the above, is what occupies *your* days (and nights?). It is no different in the educational arena.

The federal government cannot and should not compel preparatory programs or school systems to participate. What it can do is to provide incentives to take the risk of moving in new directions. The problems that will be encountered will be very thorny. I know I am being repetitious when I say that we are talking about an idea and a process that in the most explicit way will transform schools and their classrooms. We are setting sail on uncharted seas. There will be storms, maybe even hurricanes. Some programs will falter and fail. Some will succeed, at least in part. And when I say "succeed," I mean that we will gain that kind of experience on the basis of which we will have a more secure feeling about the dimensions of the problem and how we can use that experience to make the necessary improvements.

The federal government has spent many billions of dollars to support research on the etiology of cancers and on new treatments. That support was *not* based on the expectation that the knowledge we needed would give us *quickly* the answers we desperately want. Most of that research was unproductive. We have had as many fads and fashions in cancer research as in educational research. But can there be any doubt that the most sobering and yet productive outcome has been a more realistic appreciation of the complexity of the problem? My proposal is based on two assumptions: The problems in education are complex; and, once we take the big idea seriously, we will find that those problems are more complex than we thought. Murphy's law on doctoral research states that if any problem can arise, it will. Sullivan's law states that Murphy's law is a gross underestimation!

All of this is prologue to a caveat: My proposal should *not* be justified on the grounds that we know *precisely* how these programs should be implemented, and what the outcomes will be and when. It should be justified on several grounds: What we are now doing (and what we have tried) is not working; an important source of our failures has been identified; we think we know the problem; we will encounter many roadblocks, not least of which is the weight of habit and tradition; but we have no alternative to making a start on the basis of what we now know, knowing full well that what we now know will turn out to require correction.

In short, Mr. President, only *you* can begin to give the nation a realistic appraisal of what we are up against, only *you* can get the people to be wary of quick fixes, only *you* can gain their commitment to support an educational revolution, only *you* can get them to see that however understandable and well motivated past efforts have been, they were very largely failures, and only *you* can get them to see that your proposals are intended to prevent a bad situation from getting worse.

Back to FDR. Are you aware that in his first campaign for the presidency—a time when the Great Depression was picking up steam—he ran on a platform which, it turned out, was grossly misguided and insensitive to the dimensions of the catastrophe? It was not until he assumed the presidency that he realized how simplistic his conceptions had been. Fortunately, he had the courage not only to change his thinking but to tell the nation how serious the situation was. Yes, much of his New Deal was ineffective, "quick fixes" were not in short supply, but he did gain public support to think and act boldly. It should occasion no surprise that his lasting achievements were preventive in nature: social security, the environment, rural electrification, the Securities and Exchange Commission, a changed banking system, and the formal and informal ways he sought (before we entered World War II) to prevent the subjugation of Europe by Hitler and Mussolini. His opponents called him a war-mongerer. They were blind, he had 20-20 vision for what was coming down the road. He thought preventively.

Let us assume, Mr. President, that you do not cotton to my proposals. But on the basis of what you have said or written I have to assume that you know in your guts that whatever you do in regard to education must not be a carbon copy of past thinking and actions. It has to be more radical than that. As you have said numerous times, "We can no longer justify throwing money at the problem. We have to move in new and bold directions."

I have not cornered the market on new ideas. What I have called the big idea is not new. For a time at least (maybe a few seconds!) I can entertain the possibility that I am overevaluating the validity and ramifications of the big idea. Let us assume I am. The point is that for you to be the education president you want to be, you (and your advisors and, of course, the Third Lady) will have to come up with other ideas that meet this criterion: *They very explicitly will require the transformation of schools, classrooms, and preparatory programs.* Not changes or add-ons, but *transformations.*

Respectfully,

Seymour B. Sarason

XXI

Dear Mrs. Third Lady:

I knew you would respond favorably to Schaefer-Simmern's and Koch's books. You are right; you have to see what Schaefer enabled his "students" to do. I was fortunate to observe what he did: how he got each person absorbed in his or *her* imagery and in the process of giving it ordered form. The reproductions in the book speak for themselves—up to a point. There is a difference between seeing those reproductions and seeing the originals of which I have several. That is what worries me about my film proposal, i.e., it will take a high level of artistry to approximate the "real thing." I have seen loads of "teaching" films but only a few were compelling in getting me to feel I was seeing the "real thing." One of those few was a series of films of how two teachers in adjacent classrooms (same grade level) handled management problems. The contrast was the difference between day and night. If my memory serves me right, it was done by Jacob Kounin at Wayne State University at least forty years ago.

Now to your truly important question. Both for Schaefer and Koch the big idea was in and part of their psychological bloodstream. They were superb teachers. But, you ask, is it realistic to expect that most teachers could do what they were able to do? The answer is *no*. But that answer in no way suggests that most teachers cannot approximate what Schaefer and Koch did. The question is *not* whether most teachers can climb their Mt. Everest the way Schaefer and Koch climbed theirs. The question is how far up that Mt. Everest most teachers can climb. It would be mammothly insulting and unfair to imply that most teachers would be unable to leave "level ground." That very few would reach the top is predictable. However far most teachers would climb would be infinitely better than what we have now. If my proposal about preparatory programs was implemented, the teachers graduated from them should be compared to those from traditional programs. The ultimate payoff will be in that comparison. One of my critics once wrote: "Sarason is no John Dewey." I wrote to tell him that he was absolutely right. But, I asked him, was he suggesting that what I have done and written is no better or worse than what the bulk of my contemporaries do and write? If that is what he was implying, I would be glad to send him a list of eminent contemporaries who would disagree with him. He never answered my letter. May I put it this way: Sarason is to Dewey as most teachers would be to Schaefer and Koch. That *is* the case and that is satisfaction enough *for me*, as it would be for most teachers. I've done my best, as will most teachers, and none of us will leave this world unhappy with the thought that we fell short, far short, of greatness.

I'm going to risk being seen by you as presumptuous and intrusive by responding to what I sense is between the lines of your letter. What I sensed was that you thought I would look askance at presidential proposals that, if not markedly different than past ones, are essentially efforts either at repair or bulwarking a status quo to avoid further deterioration. And the reason, as you imply, for these proposals is that the President has to appear that he is responding to what people generally, and vested interests in particular, say they need and want. I understand this, which is why I would have been a disaster as a politician. It will surprise you to learn that one of my heroes is Machiavelli, the father of political science. What the world still holds against him (unjustifiably) is the way he told The Prince to understand and deal with the world as it is, not as he *wished* it was. Machiavelli wanted The Prince to change and unify Italy—to build a nation—but he pleaded with The Prince never to forget that he had opponents, he had obligations to his people, and in the final analysis he could change things only if he had the people's backing. That meant he could not always have it his way. But it also meant that he had to exploit every opportunity to bring him nearer his goal. You know what Machiavelli would say to your husband (in today's language)? "Of course you should horse trade. But you trade with your head not your heart, not to be a nice guy but a farseeing one, not to end up even (although that's not bad) but ahead, not to satisfy your ego but the vital interests of your people, not to be loved but respected." All of this is by way of saying two things: The President has to play the game, but at every step of the way he should exact that kind of support for the programs he values most. The name of the game is constituency building, and horse trading is one way of building. If this is not the best of all possible worlds—a conclusion Machiavelli considered axiomatic—let us not make it worse by misjudging what it is.

Not so incidentally, have you or the President read O'Connor's *The Last Hurrah*? Not the film, which was terrible, but the novel. I read it at least once a year. Machiavelli would have loved the novel. It was the first book I had my graduate students read.

Saying that this is not the best of all possible words does not mean you accept it. It certainly does not justify cynicism and passivity, and it in no way absolves us of the obligation to try to climb our Mt. Everests.

How on earth did I descend to this sermonizing? It's your fault! Anytime anyone asks a question or suggests that people (in this case, teachers) cannot be or do better than they are or do, I get stirred up. I'm not a historian, but I've read enough history to know that underestimating what people are and can be has been so universal and constant as to force me to consider that it must be in our genes. Fear not, I shall not give in to that kind of fatalism. When in doubt, blame genes! They can't talk back.

Respectfully,

Seymour B. Sarason

P.S. Yes, I know some of the President's advisors on education. Yes, they are bright, dedicated, knowledgeable, and decent. No, they are neither bold nor imaginative. I'm sorry to have to say that. It makes me sound conceited, arrogant, demeaning, i.e., a pompous fool. All I can say in defense is that their track record over the years doesn't come close to mine when it comes to predicting what in fact has happened and continues to happen. Are these advisors capable of being bold and imaginative? I assume they are. Why haven't they been? I'm uncomfortable with argumentum *ad hominems*. Perhaps the President should say to them: "Don't tell me only what is possible. Tell me what we must do. Assume everything is on the table. Nothing is sacred. When President Franklin Roosevelt received a letter from Albert Einstein advising the pursuit of the possibility of harnessing atomic energy for military purposes, he may not have understood the physics of the problem, but he knew he was being asked to okay something new, bold, and imaginative. Assume you are the Einsteins of the educational world. What would you say in your letters?"

P.S. You ask why I have not even alluded to modern, wondrous technology as instruments for improving educational performance. My answer is simple: *Any* technology not embedded in a context informed and organized on the basis of the big idea will be of no avail. Honesty requires that I tell you that I am probably one of a handful of people who believes that the worst thing that befell western civilization was the industrial revolution. Aside from PAM and air conditioning, it wasn't worth it! An internationally known economist (whose name I cannot recall, my Alzheimer memory was faulty from age two) wrote a book *The Harried Leisure Class*. His half-facetious theme was that from a purely economic standpoint technology intended to make life easier and more gracious is no screaming success.

XXII

Dear Mr. President:

Here is a preface to your educational message to Congress, which, as I read in the *New York Times*, you will deliver in person. To my knowledge, no president has ever done that. A very wise and bold decision.

It is no secret that one of my heroes is Pope John XXIII who convened a Vatican Council to begin the process of changing and reinvigorating the Catholic Church. That is a process I call upon you and the American people to start and engage in, in order to change and reinvigorate our schools. Just as the Pope knew that the Church was a worldwide collection of dioceses varying widely and wildly on a host of characteristics pertaining to doctrine and practice, we have to face the fact that the same is true for our thousands of school districts. Unlike a diocese, each of our school districts is autonomous, a fact that makes the attainment of a general change extraordinarily difficult in the short and long term. The word *education* is not to be found in our Constitution. Our founding fathers wisely regarded education as a local affair, not one to be controlled by a central government. There are responsibilities the federal government cannot shirk, but among them is and must *not* be the micro-managing of our schools. Desegregating schools, mainstreaming handicapped children, making funds available to inner city schools, outlawing gender discrimination—none of these and more were federal mandates for what should be taught and how in classrooms. All of these efforts were understandably based on the hope that somehow, some way, our class-rooms would become places where students willingly pursued and gained satisfaction from learning.

However sincere our efforts, however much we have spent, the fact is that our efforts have fallen far short of our expectations. That is putting a gloss on the present situation. We now know, to a degree as never before, that we are in deep, deep trouble. For all practical purposes, we have failed. Not to recognize and face up to that failure, which no one willed, is no longer possible or acceptable. We can no longer maintain the fiction that our major problem is with our urban schools. The fact is that an alarming, a frightening, a scandalously large number of all students are turned off by, not turned on by, the educational process. For too many students schooling is like medicine: They take it not because they want to but because they are forced to, even though the medicine does not make them feel better. And I need not recite here the statistics on the number of students who decide not to take the medicine.

Basic to what I shall propose is a maxim as simple as its history is long: Unless we start with "what children are and where they are," unless we start with their questions, what they are curious about, what they want to learn, we perpetuate the tradition of pouring knowledge into them and requiring them to set aside their interests, their curiosities, their wondrous, question-asking worlds. That does not mean that where we start is where we end. Our obligation, and as a society it is our most important one, is to impart our cherished values to our young, to ensure the continuity of these values, truly to conserve the best of our traditions. But it has become self-defeating of our purposes to continue to adhere to classroom practices that do not acknowledge that the pedagogical task is to meld two worlds: the world of children and our adult world. That melding has not and will not occur unless we start with and help children give expression to their worlds. Make no mistake about it, if we start where we must and should, our classrooms, the way schools are organized, the tyranny of calendar-powered, calendar-imprisoned curricula, and our criteria for performance and assessment will have to change, and dramatically so.

So where do we start? Before outlining my proposals I must caution you about several things. The first is that we avoid scapegoating school personnel, as if they willed the crisis we face. No more or less than the rest of us, they have been unwitting prisoners of ideas and practices that have been feckless. The second is that any truly radical departure from educational traditions will arouse resistance and controversy, as events in the Catholic Church after the Vatican Council well illustrate. In fact, any proposal for educational reform that does not stir resistance and controversy should be regarded as either a cosmetic or a bromide. We have had our fill of both. The third caution is that we take seriously that our goal is to change the nature of life in the classroom. The fourth is that we take primary prevention seriously, which is not to say that we eschew efforts at repair but that we make prevention of co-equal importance. In an ultimate sense prevention is infinitely more effective and less costly than a near-exclusive dependence on repair. The fifth caution is that we are dealing with problems that are not amenable to quick fixes. And, finally, there is a difference between doing what we think we can do, and what we know we *have* to do. I have decided to bite the bullet and propose what we have to do.

My initial proposal is that we begin radically to downsize our schools, especially our middle and high schools. If you accept the maxim that you begin with what children are and where they are, it follows as night follows day that you have to have the time and resources to get to know students. In too many of our schools students feel unknown, unrelated, anonymous, like particles in a cloud chamber. If it is unfair to call these schools warehouses, let us at least face up to the fact that in too many of these schools some of the major ingredients for productive learning do not exist. Can we be sure that downsizing will lead to higher levels of achievement? Maybe yes, maybe no. Is it likely that downsizing will engender in more students a sense of belonging, a sense of being respected, a sense that one counts for more than being a mere occupant of a classroom seat? The answer is yes. We do not provide meals to Head Start children because we are certain that meals mean better learning. We provide the meals because we know they need them. Similarly, students in our middle and high schools need to feel socially, interpersonally related to their peers and teachers. When such needs are not met, some of the most important ingredients for productive learning and satisfying relationships are missing.

When my First Lady was in a preparatory program for teachers, she read a book in which were these words: "If the President and Congress, in their infinite wisdom, passed a law cutting class size in half, it could not be implemented. We would be able to build twice the number of schools. We are not able to prepare twice the number of teachers, especially if quality of students and programs is taken into account." Let us not be distracted by that writer's snide remarks about the degree of our wisdom, or by his pessimistic outlook. The fact is that he is quite correct in identifying quality of would-be educators as a crucial problem about which we have done virtually nothing. But who would deny that quality of students cannot be divorced from quality of preparatory programs? Preparatory programs prepare their students for classrooms as they now are, not as they should be. And by that I mean they ill-prepare their graduates for how one starts with, and never forgets, where students are: What ideas, questions, and concerns they bring to the classroom. Teachers have been and are trained to implement a curriculum, a predetermined one, and they do this seriously and with the best of intentions. In the process they have been rendered insensitive to questions, interests, and concerns students bring to any kind of subject matter. There is abundant evidence that classrooms, generally speaking, are intellectually uninteresting places. They are not places where the world of children is as respected as the world of the adult. Not only do we not start with what and where children are, but it is as if we deliberately set out to convince children that their world is of no moment, that it has little or no role in productive learning.

Presidential addresses to Congress are not occasions for autobiography. Permit me, however, one lapse from tradition. It concerns the best teacher I ever had: my grandfather. My grandparents lived down the block from us. Because both of my parents worked, I spent a great deal of time with my grandparents. Rarely did I ever spend time with my grandfather without, at some point, his asking me: "What, son, would *you* like to know about *me*?" And since I, like every normal child, had more questions than you can shake a stick at, I kept my grandfather busy. I learned a great deal from him in terms of sheer knowledge, but the most important gift he gave me was an attitude I never verbalized until recently: Asking and pursuing questions of significance in your life keeps you alive. My grandfather never lectured me. He would start with where I was. More so than my working parents, he engendered in me the sense that I counted, that what interested me interested him, that no question or interest was off limits. I never regarded him as a teacher, but today I know how good a teacher he was and that he had a curriculum the aim of which was to meld his and my world.

I shall be submitting to you for consideration a proposal intended to stimulate and to encourage preparatory programs to prepare educators not for classrooms as they are but for what they should be: Places where they will take seriously that "pouring in" knowledge into the minds of children is to extinguish curiosity and interest. Classrooms must become places that respect the world of children, that begin with that world, and that never push that world off the classroom agenda. My proposal will also require that the schools to which these preparatory programs send their students, where these students will likely get positions, will commit themselves to make those changes that will allow teachers to apply what they have learned under conditions consistent with the requirements of the new pedagogy. My proposal will be the opposite of cosmetic because it will call for dramatic changes in how children and teachers experience and live with each other in classrooms.

Medicine today is incomprehensible unless you start with a report written over 90 years ago. It was called *Medical Education in the United States and Canada*, and it was sponsored by the Carnegie Foundation for the Improvement of Teaching. It was conducted not by a physician but by a leading educator of the day, Abraham Flexner. Compared to the quality of medical education in pre-Flexner days, the quality of public school education today is, believe it or not, superb. What Flexner did was to make a most convincing case that unless we changed what went on in medical school classrooms, laboratories, and hospitals, the public welfare was endangered. Fortunately, Flexner was the right man at the right time with the right support. Life in the medical school classroom changed forever.

I shall be submitting to you the name of an educator who will direct a study with the identical aims of the Flexner report, i.e., to make comprehensive observations of preparatory programs to determine what we must do to change how we prepare educators for an altered role in what will be altered classrooms. As long as we steer clear of changing life in the classroom, history will regard us as tinkerers. We know what needs to be done. Have we the will to do it, knowing full well that the road ahead has many potholes?

Mr. President, it is as obvious to me as it will be to you that if I had to depend for my living on being a speech writer for presidents, I would starve to death. My plea to you and your speech writers is that you do not sugarcoat the central message: *The nature of life in the classroom must change*, and if we go down that road, life in schools will change.

Respectfully,

Seymour B. Sarason

P.S. Esther has given me permission to add the following as the ending of your address. ("You will exhaust yourself, but if I say no, you'll be impossible to live with. Of all the patients I have ever had, you have been the most difficult. You have ten minutes, and no more. Believe me, I'm being very therapeutic.")

In educating our youth, what do we owe them? We want them to acquire knowledge and skills, but that is not enough. We want them to be prepared for the world of work, but that is not enough. We want them to graduate from our high schools and colleges, but that is not enough. None of these is enough unless we have, in addition, given students, implanted in them, the desire, the need, willingly to pursue over their lifetimes a deepening of their understanding of the world they live in. Is there anyone who would deny that the God-created human is a question-asking, questing, curiosity-powered organism? Is there anyone who would dispute that what distinguishes us from all other living creatures is that we are always trying, seeking, struggling to meld our pasts, presents, and futures? An educational system that does not capitalize on our uniqueness is a system that is shortchanging our youth.

Some will say I am a utopian, that what I want for our youth is beyond the capabilities of most of them. That is a criticism always leveled by those against any view that challenged the so-called conventional wisdom about human nature and capabilities. In accord with the best of our national traditions, I, and I am sure you, stand for the highest standards, ideals, and expectations. Our task is not to proclaim them but to create those conditions that will permit more of our youth to meet those standards, ideals, and expectations.

P.S. It took 20 minutes but my beloved Esther could say nothing because she was on the phone with our beloved Julie.

P.S. I'm giving thought to a letter about a proposal I made 25 years ago. It was a proposal about *adult* education, about which a number of people have written, but about which there has been little action.

XXIII

Dear Mrs. Third Lady:

I assume you read my "message," and I also assume that you, like me, concluded I am not a speech writer.

What bothers me is that I did not adequately articulate one of my strongest beliefs, one that has been bedrock to everything I have thought, done, and written. It is best illustrated by the work of Schaefer-Simmern and Koch. What they (and others) demonstrated is the power of the belief that there usually is a tremendous gulf between what people do and *what they can learn to do.* What makes a teacher great is that he or she creates the conditions in which people learn to do something of which they and others thought them to be incapable. "You are capable of more than you think"—that is the belief with which great teachers start. Our schools—and it is true of schools in every other country—start with preconceptions of what children are, what they are capable of, and those preconceptions have very little to do with potentialities and a great deal to do with what I will call perceived realities. I know the rhetoric: "We want to help each child realize his or her full potential." And that is said sincerely, blind to the fact that our classrooms are not organized to allow teachers or students to plumb that potential. Inevitably we start with preconceptions. That is in the nature of things. What is not in that nature is the recognition that preconceptions are *always* a reflection of place and era (among other things). Different eras, different preconceptions. Isn't that the obvious lesson to be drawn from the history of women, minorities, handicapped people, and aged people (like me)? Great teachers challenge preconceptions, and so do great schools—of which we have pitifully few.

Why is it that everybody regards it as self-evident, essential, and absolutely crucial that our schools should help students understand and utilize science and technology? How can you challenge such a goal? Let us leave aside the fact that what passes for science education is what adults consider important, not what students are curious about, e.g., why is the sky blue, why does an airplane stay in the sky, how come we can hear voices on the telephone, what makes a car move, why do we have earthquakes, what makes for thunder and lightening, why does a bullet travel so fast—you can go on and on listing "scientific and technological" questions in the heads of children. But who starts with, capitalizes on, and is vigilant about "their" questions? It should not really be set aside because we have to own up to how well we have made science *uninteresting*. But aside we shall set it. And we shall also set aside the equally obvious fact that the wondrous achievements of science and technology have not made us (or the rest of the world) happier or safer. What we shall not set aside is the fact that most people (white-black, rich-poor) are poignantly aware that they do not get the satisfaction, the sense of fulfillment, from their work that they had expected. They feel unused, or underused, or empty. I have argued (as others have long before me) that our inability or unwillingness to take seriously that from our earliest days we seek and engage in creative—artistic—activity, to put our personal stamp on what we create or do, has robbed people of a most important source of personal accomplishment and satisfaction. Indeed, our schools, which reflect our society, have always regarded education in the arts as a frill or luxury. Expendable.

Let me put it this way: Assume that at the point of a gun you have to choose between (a) selecting and supporting the Schaefer-Simmerns and Kochs as teachers in our schools or (b) their counterparts in science. You *have* to choose between the two. Most people would respond by saying the choice is easy: How can you compare the importance of science education to that of arts education? Ridiculous. That, Mrs. Third Lady, is the way most people and, therefore, educators would respond. Looking into the barrel of a gun, I would opt for the Schaefer-Simmerns and Kochs of this world. No, it is not self-evident to me that science education should be given exalted status. It is self-evident to me that education in the arts and sciences is co-equal in importance. As long as we consign education in the arts to the "it's nice but not truly crucial" category, we will continue to be prisoners of preconceptions that blind us to potentialities we in our earliest years exploited but which schooling extinguished or pushed "underground."

Forgive me. I have regressed to my teaching years. Maybe it is because you and the President have been an audience for me, and I could not resist "professing." Frankly, what I think explains my struggle in this and the previous letter is a plaguing feeling of loneliness, the sense that so few people today can even entertain the possibility that we are far from understanding and capitalizing on the potentials of the human organism. We like to think, as every past era has, that we have gone beyond those who came before us, i.e., we are more knowledgeable, more in control of nature, more in control of our own destiny, and, of course, wiser. And all of that adds up to "progress." Then why are we in such a mess? Why that sense of a failed promise, of a vanished optimism that was uniquely American, of a society out of control, of an educational system that is not working? Why was your husband willing to take the gargantuan risk to tell the American people (as Churchill told his people) that he did not seek the presidency to preside over the demise of the United States? Why did the people elect him, instead, as has usually been the case, of shooting the messenger of bad news? Why are they so ready to support not just change but *drastic* change? That is why I began to write to the President. He was the first president to say that changing our schools is his (by far) top priority. That is a real first. I felt I had to use whatever energy I have to try to be helpful. That is why my letters have been like a broken record: We have to change our schools, but if that is not preceded or accompanied by a change in our thinking, in our preconceptions, in how we regard what and where children are, in our imaginativeness and boldness—absent these changes and we will again confirm the maxim that the more things change the more they remain the same.

Respectfully,

Seymour B. Sarason

P.S. It would be correct to say that I feel not lonely but alone in an intellectual sense. As long as I have Esther, I can't be lonely. When I read this letter to her, she became reflective and then said, "Science is overrated, the arts less so, but you said nothing about love. They've put everything but love in the curriculum, which is quite an omission. But if love were in the curriculum, it would end up being uninteresting."

P.S. Of all the books I have written—and there are those who feel I have written too many—I have a favorite: *The Challenge of Art to Psychology*. A better title would have been: *The Status of Artistic Activity as a Barometer of a Society's Worth*. That is too much of a mouthful! Periclean Athens and renaissance Florence (really Italy) are not monuments in human history by chance.

P.S. It is too easy to blame educators for the inadequacies of our schools. And it is too easy to conclude that schools can be *the* vehicle to change our society. If only it were so simple! That is why it is so important for the President to challenge the people to understand that schools will truly change when the larger society changes its preconceptions and can essentially say, "Let the revolution begin." Yes, if the President can get the people to agree that "we have met the enemy and it is us," the revolution will have started. Revolutions are messy, complicated affairs. But no more so than a slow, steady deterioration in what has been distinctive and best in our ideals, values, and goals. There are times when I dearly hope there is a hereafter. It is at those times that I have the fantasy that I will meet the founding fathers of our country and I am permitted to address them on what they deliberately omitted from the constitution, i.e., education. They, of course, have been able to witness what has happened since they wrote that literally unique document. What will be their response? Needless to say, the fantasy ends with thunderous applause from an audience about whom it could never be said that they knew the price of everything and the value of nothing. Values, ideas, and ideals—they were not in doubt that history would judge them by how consistent and courageous they would be in regard to those factors. A new fantasy now occupies me: The President calls for a constitutional convention to rethink, reformulate, and rewrite the place and function of schooling in America. Just as the 1787 convention was necessary to correct the dangers and inadequacies of the Articles of Confederation, this one would have an analogous charge. The Constitutional Convention did *not* amend the Articles of Confederation. It produced a new document reflective of new ideas, a new vision, and the expectation that the citizenry would live up to its new commitments. It asked the best from the people, no less and no more. Far from being wide-eyed, up-in-the-clouds utopians, they were the most realistic, courageous, responsible group in human history.

P.S. Esther has agreed to allow me to write a book called *The Collected Sermons of Seymour Sarason*. With one proviso: She will write, and I will not edit, her introduction. My reply was, "When I want the truth, I will ask you for it. No thanks." The world can do without that book.

XXIV

Dear Mrs. Third Lady:

You are very astute! Yes, I have said nothing about a national testing-assessment program and vouchers. I am well aware that the President is being pressured to support such programs. The fact is that I twice started to write to both of you about my views. I gave up for two reasons. The first is that I got (and get) too upset. (I do have limitations and vulnerabilities, personal and intellectual!) A national testing-assessment program has a surface plausibility that, in these days of "quality control in education" appeals to people, some of whom should know better. For example, such a program would be identical in purpose to similar programs already in place in a number of states. Connecticut has had a state-wide program for years. Before that program was instituted the largest cities in the state (New Haven, Hartford, Bridgeport, and Waterbury) had inadequate schools, i.e., their local testing programs showed their students to be doing very poorly on achievement tests. It was true that these cities tended to keep these results from public scrutiny. Enter the hard-nosed "reformers" who said that a state-wide, state-mandated program would not only establish— objectively, comprehensively, periodically, publicly— the school achievement of all students but would morally serve as a stimulus for communities to improve the quality of education. The truth shall set you free! How could a school system and the community it serves avoid doing whatever needed to be done to improve the average level of school achievements? It was a variant of the "shape up or ship out" mentality.

So what happened? Ten or more years later the schools that were doing poorly are (the usual few exceptions aside) still doing poorly. In fact, from what I know about the New Haven school system the situation is worse. (My counterintelligence about the New Haven school system is not what it used to be, but it is still active and revealing.) Let us assume, charitably, that it is no worse. How do we explain this? How do those in the school system explain it? True to my hedgehog genes I explain it by the simple fact that *virtually nothing has changed in how children experience classrooms.* Yes, they have put computers in almost every classroom, they have changed curricula (read "books"), they have made token gestures (I am being charitable) to giving more responsibility to teachers, they certainly and discernibly increased teacher salaries, and they made the schools safer places for students and teachers. They get an A for effort and a D- for performance.

How do school personnel explain it? Their answers are several: Children are not motivated; their family life works against, not for, educational achievement; too many children have too many problems; administrators feel teachers are not creative, and teachers feel that administrators are incapable of being helpful; and when economic recession reared its ugly head and class size increased, several personnel had a ready explanation. No one says or even suggests that *maybe* a large part of the problem is the "pouring-in tradition" which means that classrooms are places where students are taught (i.e., told) what is good for their souls even though it is obvious that most of them don't want their souls saved in that way.

A word about my counterintelligence network that today consists of two dear (younger) friends who teach in the New Haven schools. They are very atypical in that years ago they read some of my books, sought me out, and even sat in on my Yale seminars. They become hedgehogs for which I am sorry because it has made life difficult for them. They try valiantly—God do they try! —to take the big idea seriously, but they are so pressured by the calendar-determined curriculum and by knowing they will be judged by how their [elementary] students do on the state-mandated tests. By the spring of the year they are dispirited, angry, disillusioned, and exhausted. We get together about once a month to dispense therapy to each other. Not so incidentally, what these friends bemoan, and what they say other teachers bemoan, is the *complete* absence of the sense of community in their schools. As I know from years of personal experience, schools are not places where ideas are discussed. It is not that school personnel are incapable of such discussions. It is rather that they do not see the point of such discussions, i.e., ideas are not part of the school agenda, they will be perceived as disruptive forms of whistle-blowing, they will literally be fruitless. So each teacher retreats and accommodates to what is expected, not to what needs to be done. *School faculty meetings have organization and purpose identical to those of the relationships between students and teachers in classrooms.* Teachers experience in faculty meetings what students do in classrooms: Information is poured into them, they are receptacles for "knowledge."

Some thoughts about ideas. My teacher friends think very highly of me. Even though I think they overevaluate what I have written, at this stage of my life I am not about to look a gift horse in the mouth. From time to time they ask me, "Why is it that no one in the New Haven schools knows your work, although some have heard your name?" Over the years I met with scores of groups of school personnel around the country. On each occasion I have been introduced as someone who has written a lot on education. I never had reason to believe that (the usual few exceptions aside) anyone in the audience had ever read anything I had written or had ever heard about me. When my friends ask their question, my standard reply is, "The important question is not why they have not read or heard about me, but why they have not read others, during and before my time, whose ideas represent the most serious challenge to the *Status quo*, ideas that go far to explain longstanding, intractable problems in education. I have been a conveyor of their ideas, not the source of origin. At best, I reinvented their intellectual wheels."

The preparation of educators does not, to indulge understatement, pay other than lip service to ideas. The reasons for that are complex and historical and they are wrapped up (for me) in this question: Why is the field of education a second, or third, or even a non-citizen in our colleges and universities? There is another question: Why is the imagery that people have of teachers, classrooms, and schools so superficial, so devoid of an appreciation of the ingredients of productive learning, so blind to what and where children are, so reflective of the belief that education is what you put into kids and *not* how you meld their and our worlds? Schools are a reflection of our society. Let us not scapegoat the educators. The puzzling question is why there are *any* educators who know the game and the score and have to settle for a raincheck to be used in their next reincarnation.

So, again, where do you start to stop this vicious cycle? As I said in an earlier letter: You start with the preparatory programs for educators. It will not be easy. It will take a long, long time. It has the disadvantage of not being a quick fix. We will make mistakes. But we will be dealing with important issues.

A national testing assessment program? What a distraction! What a misdiagnosis. What a clear example of learning nothing from past experience. What a marvelous way of guaranteeing that, more than in the past, classrooms will be places where students will "learn" facts and skills and that their worlds will increasingly be off limits. Isn't it surprising that proponents of the program never (but never) say anything about possible, negative side effects, or can imagine unintended consequences, or indicate that they are aware of the minuscule improvements (if any) of state-mandated programs? With "cures" like that you never have to worry about a decrease in chronic, educational disease.

I'm getting upset. Not really. Just plain frustrated, and worried that the American genes for biting the bullet, for institutional revolution, seem to be in short supply. It seems that the only times these genes appear is when there is a Great Depression or a foreign threat to our security and traditions.

My warmest regards
to both of you,

Seymour B. Sarason

P.S. My next letter will be about vouchers. It will be a short letter (famous last words).

P.S. As someone who was in a preparatory program and then a teacher for several years, how do you react to what I have said about programs and ideas? *Please, please* respond *candidly*. Don't worry about *my* feelings. I may be quite old, but I can still learn from others.

XXV

Dear Mr. and Mrs. President:

Someone said that it is hard to be completely wrong. The passionate partisans of vouchers are an exception. Vouchers make no sense unless certain assumptions are valid:

1. There are enough first-class schools to accommodate all who would choose them. *That is nonsense, sheer nonsense.* However you define a first-class school—getting agreement on that is a problem in itself—they are few in number.

2. Vouchers would serve as a goad to inadequate schools to improve the education they now provide. The great bulk of these schools have been intractable to improvement as a consequence of myriad past efforts. Why should vouchers have a different fate? The answer given by the partisans is as simple as it is superficial: The need to *compete* will be more effective than any of the past efforts. The assumption is that competition will force schools and their communities to appropriate funds to obtain the resources and personnel necessary to permit them to be competitive. If we have learned anything in the past half century, it is that money will not buy you quality education. Let us leave aside that many communities will be unable to come up with such increased funding. Let us ask: Why are these schools inadequate? Is it, as the partisans seem to imply, that school personnel are stupid, unimaginative, uncaring, unmotivated, i.e., they are, if not *the* cause, a major cause of the inadequacies? I have been in too many of these schools to accept such an explanation. It is far more complex than that. I can point to a few instances where new leadership in such a school brought about improvement, but those leaders (principals) did so not because of their formal preparation but because they had ideas and vision they acquired God knows where.

And one of those ideas was what I have called the big idea: You had to start where children *and* teachers are with their buried ideas and hopes. What the advocates for vouchers completely ignore is the role of preparatory programs for teachers and administrators. And by ignoring that they are ignoring a problem that contributes mightily to the inadequacies of schools. A voucher program would be adding insult to injury to these inadequate schools. Vouchers are a variety of the quick fix for *some* children (more of this in a moment) and a misguided poor fix for schools generally.

3. Inadequate schools are *not* a separate species as the voucher advocates seem to assume. They differ only in degree from other schools, they are at a different point on a continuum. I came to know "good" schools. And what is a good school, e.g., a high school? It is a place where most students graduate and go to college. I came to know some of these "good" high schools. And what characterizes many of their students is their disinterest in ideas in the larger world in which they live, a sheer lack of curiosity about our past, TV is where they get their kicks, newspapers are important because they tell you what is playing in the movies, and books are in libraries to which they rarely go. Their knowledge and interest in our world are minuscule. So much for good schools. I know I sound old fashioned, a relic from the past, a cynic, a disillusioned old man unwilling or unable to accept change, one who has nostalgia for the good old days which, they will say, were not all that good. Yes, they were not all that good except, speaking only for myself, that I learned from different people in different ways (in and out of schools and the university) that I had an obligation to learn as much as I could about myself and my (our) world. Not an obligation to enjoy life but "to make something of yourself." It was an obligation that has served me well. Am I to be criticized for wanting to provide to our young people those educational contexts and opportunities that gave meaning to my life? Am I wrong in saying that if you want to get the best out of them, you provide the best liberating education you can. You don't start by lowering your sights. You give the best to get the best. So much for too many of our "good" schools. End of sermon.

4. When vouchers became a fashionable idea, Esther, our two young teacher friends, and I performed an "exercise." We started with this question: What are, by *conventional* standards, the good schools in the larger New Haven area? Initially, we asked that question only in regard to New Haven schools, but we could only agree on a handful of schools, so we enlarged the geographical area. We came up with twelve schools. We then asked this question: If you lived in the New Haven ghetto, what problems would you have enrolling your "voucher" child or children in these schools? (Let us assume, as we did, that ghetto parents would have ways of distinguishing between good and bad schools, a very shaky assumption for *any* parent.) The first and most obvious problem would be transportation because most of the schools were not in New Haven. If the father and mother had one car, they would probably need another, unless the father and the child got up very early in the morning not only to deposit the child at school but for the father to get to work. In that case, how could the working father pick the child up in mid-afternoon? If it were a single-parent family, the mother working, how could she pick the child up? If they had more than one "voucher" child—one in an elementary school, one in a middle or high school—the problem would be even more thorny. The long and short of our exercise was the realization that for ghetto families vouchers would be grossly impractical and, of course, discriminatory. But the icing on this cake of impracticality was that vouchers (then) would be between $1,000 and $1,500, far below what non-New Haven schools charged out-of-town residents. (The private schools in the larger New Haven area then charged approximately $6,000 tuition.) Someone once said that we live in a democracy in which a Rockefeller and a welfare family have the equal right to sleep under the same bridge. Need I say more?

Back to competition. For all practical purposes, there is little competition among preparatory programs for educators. My earlier proposal to you to provide incentives to these programs to change radically how they prepare students for the realities of our schools would have the desirable effect of introducing a degree of competition among them.

Why haven't these programs changed? Why should they change? What would be appropriate incentives to change? What are the moral imperatives for them to change? Those were the questions that Abraham Flexner asked in 1909 in regard to the deplorable, if not scandalous, nature of medical education. He answered those questions, and the rest is history. Flexner was not interested in retooling the physicians of his time, although he was not opposed to it. He had, so to speak, a one-track mind: unless and until we change the preparatory education of physicians, we will be unable to capitalize on what is known about the repair and prevention of illness and disease. He wanted to prepare better "healers," but he was never in doubt that the preventive orientation was far better for the public welfare.

> Esther and I send you our
> warmest and best wishes,

> Seymour B. Sarason

P.S. This morning's TV showed you getting in a helicopter to go to Camp David where you will be drafting your educational message, which you give in two weeks. I like the way you answered the reporter who asked if your educational proposals would cost a lot of money. "The problem is not the amount of money but how willing the nation will be to support moving in new directions. My job is to convince the people that tinkering is off limits. They are ready to hear that, and I am certain they will be supportive." Your batting average just went sky high.

XXVI

Dear Mrs. Third Lady:

It was inconceivable to me that you would not agree with what I have said about preparatory programs for educators. I did not know that the program you were in was in one of the most prestigious universities in the land. You put it very well: "As students, we knew we were in a galaxy of stars. They were brilliant, stimulating people. But once I became a teacher—on my own, the door to my classroom closed, faced with a bewildering array of students, my lesson plan clear in my head, prepared to do justice to the curriculum, and assumed that every student couldn't wait for learning to start, that of course they would be cooperative and respectful—I realized how I had been programmed to be an intellectual drill sergeant who had a limited amount of time to pour the curriculum into them." I could have well used those words in some of my books. But what I treasure even more are your words: "By the end of the second month of my first year of teaching I realized that I was approaching the students in precisely the same way my teaching supervisors had approached me, i.e., I was a conveyor of pre-digested rules, facts, and techniques who no longer had to think for myself." Your letter made my week, which at my advanced age is one hell of a long time!

You are the *only* person—believe me, I have no need whatsoever to ingratiate myself to you, to gain your favor, I am way past that kind of interpersonal game—who has directed to me *the* question that is a kind of Achilles heel in my argument. My answer is in several parts:

1. If we have identified the problem, we have no alternative to devising ways to do something about it. I have always known that for any one problem there is more than

one way to approach it. But one thing I am certain about: It cannot be done by fiat, an eleventh commandment that says "Thou shalt change!" That is why I emphasized in my proposal to the President that there must be *incentives* to change.

2. When I was active (i.e., when I could travel) I came to know many faculty members of preparatory programs. In my typically nonendearing way I made clear why I thought these programs were inadequate, especially the lip service they paid to the big idea. Some of these academics, a minority, saw me as an arrogant, presumptuous, Yale professor whose assumption of the role of biblical prophet passing judgment on educational evil was proof positive of a tendency to delusions of grandeur. I can't resist telling you what a newly minted academic said to me over a lunch *to which he had invited me*. Paraphrased it went like this: "You don't know shit from Shinola about education." Paraphrased, my response was: "With dear friends like you, education need never worry about enemies." The important point is that a fair number of faculty agreed with my criticisms and defended themselves by saying that they were so constricted by state regulations, by the pressures from school administrators to give them "good, traditional teachers," by the disparity between the number of students and the number of faculty, by the low prestige preparatory programs for teachers (discernibly lower than programs for administrators) were accorded in colleges and universities, by the lack of support for innovation and risk taking—all of these and more required faculty "to play it safe, don't rock the boat, don't alienate the hands that feed you."

3. I would pose for them this question: "If you were starting from scratch and you could develop what you consider a semi-ideal program, would it look like the program you now have?" That question *always* engendered derisory laughter. That does not mean that I would agree with what they would come up with, but it sure as hell means that although they feel constrained to maintain the *status quo*, they wish it were otherwise.

4. I do not think I am overestimating the number of faculty who are dissatisfied with their programs. But even if I am, you start with where you can start, with programs

that will say, "We have to change. We want to change. Help us create the conditions permitting us to innovate, to take risks, to learn from success *and* failure."

5. What has been missing is a voice, a national voice, a Flexner-like voice, a *presidential* voice that says to official-dom in our colleges and universities, "No more can educa-tion be a second-class citizen in our universities. No more demeaning. no more scapegoating. No more business as usual. As seats of learning, research, and exploration; as the one place in our society where the tradition is that tradition is both our ally and foe; as the place where experimentation and imaginativeness are rightfully treasured, our universi-ties *must* create the conditions which will dramatically, not cosmetically, begin the process by which future generations of educational practitioners will be better prepared to par-ticipate in an educational revolution. If the new directions are not well charted, if we will make mistakes, if we will meet obstacles and resistance, so be it. But at least you will know that history will not judge you as having been so passive, so traditional, so unimaginative as to have colluded in the deterioration of our schools and, therefore, our society."

Words are dull brass to express my appreciation of your letter, i.e., of *you*. I feel less intellectually alone. John Kennedy appointed his brother Robert as attorney general. Would your husband be willing to appoint you as secretary of education? That question requires no answer. Again, thanks.

Appreciatively,

Seymour B. Sarason

P.S. In light of what I said above about preparatory pro-grams and universities, I went back and read the letter I wrote to you and the President. May I add one thing to my sermon: "If the new directions are uncharted, there is a conceptual-action compass that will not permit us to stray far from five goals. It is a compass that directs us to change the nature of relationships between faculty of these programs and educators-to-be, between classroom teachers and their students, between teachers and administrators, among teachers, and between school personnel and parents. Those are not unrealistic goals. They are necessary goals if we are to get out of the educational cosmetic business."

P.S. Yes, we cannot do less than our best to get the best out of students and educators. That is why I have been viewed by some people as a perfectionist, as someone who will not settle for doing less than we know we should do. I am seen like the Jewish grandmother who was watching her two-year-old grandson playing where the ocean beach meets the water. It was a gorgeous day. Suddenly everything turned black, there was horrendous lightening and thunder, and ten seconds later the day is again gorgeous. Except that the grandson has disappeared. The grandmother looks to the heavens and angrily berates God for his capricious and unjust action. "How", she shouts, "can you do that to someone like me who has devoutly obeyed all of your laws?" She really gave God a torrent of what-fors and how-comes. In the midst of all this, and as suddenly as before, everything turns black, lightening and thunder are heard again, and after ten seconds the day becomes gorgeous again. And there is her grandson playing at water's edge. She runs over to him, examines him closely, looks up to the heavens and says to God: "But there was a hat!" Yes, Mrs. Third Lady, I am not one who easily accepts compromises. Especially when the welfare of people is at stake. When mountain climbers are asked why they try to scale Mt. Everest, they reply "Because it is there." Analogously, when someone (like me) has a vision of what the top of the educational mountain looks like, what it should look like, is it being a sourpuss to want to reach the pinnacle? Granted that we will not reach the pinnacle. But what is a heaven for?

XXVII

Dear Dr. Cory:

Would I consider it an intrusion if you wrote to me? No, a thousand times no! When I began to inundate the President with my letters, I hoped that he would show them to his advisors on education. My fear was that my letters would get short shrift because they were so radical and repetitive. Broken record Sarason! And by short shrift I mean that although his advisors probably knew of my writings, and even agreed with them, they would be regarded as (at the least) politically impractical, i.e., they require adopting a too long-term, preventive perspective. And, as you say in your letter, the implications of my proposals will engender a lot of resistance in a lot of groups in and out of education. Do you remember what happened ten years ago when the national debt reached galactic proportions but nobody—neither Presidents Reagan and Bush or their Democratic opponents— had the guts to say right out loud what needed to be done because they knew well the oxen of diverse groups would be gored? Be nonspecific, be soporific, trot out the cliches, dig deep into the bag of gimmicks, and make like you are uttering a new Emancipation Proclamation for schools. So things got worse. My predictions held up at the same time my depression deepened.

My depression did not lessen as I read your letter until I got to your postscript. Then I knew why you wrote me. Anyone who did his graduate work with John Goodlad would cotton to my ideas. After all, John was the only one besides me who saw that unless and until we totally redesigned preparatory programs for educators, we would be treading water, getting exhausted, and ultimately drown.

I have always felt sorry for John because although he is perceived as a luminary in the educational establishment— accorded all kinds of honors and recognition, and deservedly so—the educational fraternity never really got behind him. He was and is a general with few troops. I was never a general, and I had *no* troops. Being at Yale, which is as hospitable to the field of education as the Arctic is to swimmers, my only weapon was writing.

Did John ever tell you the first time we talked with each other? It was back in the sixties (I think) and not long after Ken Davidson, Burton Blatt, and I had published our book *The Preparation of Teachers: An Unstudied Problem in Education*. John was dean of the UCLA School of Education. The phone rings and it is John Goodlad. Would I consider moving from Yale? In the abstract the answer was yes. John had already built one of the best schools of education in the country. If I went to UCLA, I would be with people committed to the field of education and, of course, with John. Did I ever agonize about what to do! The decisive factor against going to UCLA was that Esther's and my parents (in Brooklyn and Newark) were dependent on us in numerous ways, and neither of us could be commuters between the coasts. It was not that I was unhappy at Yale but rather that I felt so intellectually alone. (I sometimes suspect I wanted it that way.)

Forgive me, you did not write to stimulate my store of memories. You wanted me to know that the President had passed on my letters to his educational advisors with the charge to come up with legislation that would reflect the big idea. The problem, you say, is that it is not at all clear how you go from the big idea to the concreteness or specificity that legislation requires. You say that my proposal for the development of compelling films has been warmly embraced because the technology to make them already exists and arranging to make them will have its problems although they are far from insuperable. But how do you write legislation the intention of which requires preparatory programs "to heal themselves." If these programs are part of the problem, why should anyone expect them to come up with "solutions"? My reply is in two parts.

The first is that we are not dealing with a problem that has a "solution" in the sense that four divided by two equals two is a solution. There is more than one way of thinking and proceeding, and I do not know them all. I have not cornered the market on "ways." I have opinions, strong opinions, but I do not confuse opinions with conclusions derived from the crucible of experience. That is not true, which brings me to the second part of my reply.

What is absolutely crucial is that the need for and the substance of change have to gain *currency*, by which I mean that they have to be presented to and discussed with representatives of *all* major vested interests: directors of preparatory programs, college and university officials, teacher and administrator unions, foundations funding educational change, relevant accrediting agencies, state departments of education, and by private sector leaders. And by "presented and discussed" I mean two things: The President is *committed* to doing *something* to facilitate change in these programs consistent with the big idea, and he needs to hear from these diverse groups whatever reactions and advice they have. The President's position should be unambiguous. "I am committed to these changes. They are long overdue. All of us have been part of the problem. There are no villains. What I need is advice about how to provide incentives to those programs willing to experiment, to move in new directions. We in Washington have no intention of foisting anything on any program. Our intention is to help programs ready to depart from past practices. What would be appropriate and realistic incentives? By what criteria should we judge whether these programs should be supported? How do we avoid supporting cosmetic changes? Where are the booby traps?"

I am sure you get the point, which at its root is political in the best sense of the term: to inform and develop a supportive constituency, not only by "telling" them where *you* stand but also by actions expressing your respect for their ideas and experience. That is how ideas gain increased currency, get changed, and gain support. *In brief, in approaching these vested interests—I do not use vested here as a pejorative—you take the big idea seriously, i.e., you start with where they are, with what they have been thinking in the quiet of their nights, with their questions, with their dreams, with what they have wanted to do but could not.* If you have had any doubt about what I mean when I call myself a hedgehog, those italicized words should dispel that doubt. Do unto others what you would have others do unto you! That is basically the big idea—in the classroom, in life in general.

I am not describing a "selling" job as if you have a finished product you want people to buy. You have an idea, you are committed to it, but you know that the idea has to be mulled over, digested, assimilated, and made part of people's thinking and actions. They have to have a sense of ownership, not a sense of being dictated to, harassed, and derogated. Of course some will be allergic to the idea and will say no thank you. But there will be others who will be grateful for the opportunity to change their lives, those of their students, and those of school children.

National revolutions occur *after* a period of rising expectations. And that is what I am advocating, a process whereby expectations rise. It is a personally and intellectually demanding process, a tortuous one requiring the patience of a Job, a process the intended outcomes of which will only become clear, if they become clear at all, over decades. There will be intended and unintended consequences. So what else is new? May I suggest that you read John Dewey's *The Quest for Certainty*? In that magnificent book Dewey demonstrates that, no less than in science, the arena of our most important social problems has to be understood and judged by the maxim that the more you know the more you need to know.

I am most grateful for your letter. In these, my not-so-golden years (physically only), I can use letters that make me think. If you run into John Goodlad, please give him my best wishes. I don't know what he is up to these days. Frankly, for the past several years my reading has been restricted to rereading. John Dewey, William James, Alfred North Whitehead, Plato, Montesquieu, and the sports section of the *New York Times*. I don't have to read the other sections of that paper because Esther reads them (damn near every word), gets upset, and insists on telling me what she has read. With a wife like Esther I am in no danger of being ignorant of current examples of man's inhumanity to man. Her capacity to remain interested in the goings on in this world amazes me. Please intrude again.

Cordially,

Seymour B. Sarason
Professor of Psychology Emeritus
Yale University

P.S. Reading between the lines of your letter, I infer that you are less optimistic than I about the number of educators (in and out of preparatory programs) disposed to react favorably to proposals for radical change. If we do differ it may be because what I learned over the decades was based on talking *privately and confidentially* with hundreds (thousands?) of teachers, administrators, and faculty of preparatory programs. A surprising number, albeit a minority, expressed in crystal clear English the belief that preparatory programs needed an overhaul, i.e., a lot of things needed to be changed and preparatory programs were high on the list. But another source of my estimate is the number of people who wrote to me after reading something I had written. And several times a year I would get long-distance calls from people who thanked me for saying out loud conclusions they had already arrived at but were in no position to articulate, let alone serve as a basis for storming the barricades. One such person was Ed Meyer down in Fairfield county in Connecticut. Amongst other things in a long career, Ed taught chemistry in one of the most affluent high schools in America, i.e., the conventional "good" school. (When he graduated from *the* Bronx High School of Science, he was the valedictorian.) Ed began to write to me the way I have to the President. We became good friends. If Ed did not storm the barricades, he certainly directed a lot of intellectual bullets at those who manned them. To the administrators of his school he was a superb science teacher. Predictably, they also regarded him as a stormy petrel, a whistle-blower, a pain in the neck of routine. (I regret I never wrote him up for publication.) When Ed retired—he had had his fill—he was serendipitously in the position where, for the purposes of a market research firm, he talked on the phone to people in *all* walks of life. Since Ed is no less a hedgehog than I in matters educational, he would not terminate a phone interview until he inquired about how the person viewed our schools. He did one other thing: He began to write to leading people in education, either criticizing something they had said or written, or posing questions he requested they answer. Ed would send me carbons of letters sent and received, and at least twice a week he would relate to me over the phone (sometimes in person) what he had learned. What conclusions did I (we) draw from his experiences? The first is that the *depth* of dissatisfaction with our schools was blatant. The second was that among educators there was recognition that preparatory programs should be improved although, the usual exceptions aside, their suggestions were either superficial, or mindless, or cosmetic. The important point is that all of these educators agreed that until these programs "improved" our schools would continue downhill. That view was universal among noneducators, but they were at sea when Ed asked them what should be done. Now, you could argue from this, as I think you do, that people are not ready for radical change. I would argue that they *would* be ready—at least a significant number of them—if (and only if) a presidentially led, national forum would articulate a new vision of how educators should be prepared for the realities of our schools and communities. Not trained (as in obedience schools for dogs), but prepared for how to think about and act consistently in regard to the big idea. I am surprised that I sound like an optimist. It is not a stance with which I am comfortable! End of seminar.

P.S. I hope the President's advisors are not viewing his wife as *just* the First Lady. She knows the game and the score.

P.S. Of course I will be watching the President give his address. Not only watch but record. We finally had to succumb to the very mixed blessings of technological progress because our daughter and son-in-law recently presented us with a VCR for our 57th wedding anniversary. We have hardly used it but we will for the President's address.

P.S. I will send you a carbon of my next letter to the President. It will not be about the education of children but about adults: those who have finished their formal education, regardless of amount. I not only want to save our children but the rest of the population as well. Grandiosity becomes Sarason!

P.S. I will *not* send you a carbon. I promised the President confidentiality. I hope he will pass it on to you and other advisors. My immodest view of that letter is that it will be a blockbuster in terms of its societal implications. Whether I can do justice to my ideas in a letter is doubtful. I once wrote a book (back in the seventies) about those ideas *Work, Aging, and Social Change,* the worst possible title I could have chosen, which explains (only in part) why that book went out of mind and print very quickly. How to summarize those ideas in a letter—to the President no less—is a task that loquacious, rambling, didactic, professorial me is finding agonizingly difficult. I may decide to chuck the idea. Decisions, decisions, decisions!

XXVIII

Dear Mr. President:

You are a most unusual human being, a species not in abundance. It never occurred to me that you would send me a copy of your address. It came yesterday p.m., and I read it at least three times, as did Esther. Even so, we watched you deliver your address as if we had never read it.

Saying that you are unusual is *not* because you saw fit to use some of my ideas. Rather it stems from the fact that, in my experience at least, adhering to the *conventional* rules of courtesy and social graciousness is not a characteristic normally distributed in the population. Sometime in my middle years I woke up to the obvious: Too many people were too absorbed in pursuing their goals to discharge the obligation to recognize in some way those who in small or large degree tried to be helpful to them, even if that help or advice were not all that consequential. What do you *owe* someone who is in *your* service?

I am not saying it right. I am being too narrow. Let me put it this way: What became obvious to me was that the much maligned (or laughed at) Emily Post "rules" for social conduct had several functions. The first is to remind us that other people have feelings and expectations that deserve recognition and response. The second is a way of controlling or not playing into or exacerbating *their or our* negative or ambivalent feelings. And the third function, implied in the second, is that we accept the obligation to accord others what we want them to accord us: worth, recognition, civility. Without "rules" life is more of a jungle than it need be. You can sum up all of Emily Post in one sentence: *You do not take people's feelings and expectations for granted.*

You did not *have* to send me your address. You and the Third Lady did not *have* to reply to any of my letters in the way the two of you did. The fact is that I never expected to receive other than a form letter from you, which would have been in the "letter but not the spirit" of Emily Post. If you will go back to my first letter, and read between the lines, you will find that I was not sanguine about the depth or seriousness of your understanding of our educational crisis. Essentially, what I said to you was, "I would like to believe your campaign words meant something, but I have heard the speeches of too many presidents to believe other than 'deep down inside he is shallow.'" You did not play into my frustrations, disappointments, pessimism. That is why I regard you and the Third Lady as unusual. End of this "bourgeois, middle-class" sermon!

It was quite an address. You presented the prevention theme in a clear, compelling way. The challenge you laid down to colleges and universities in regard to changing preparatory programs—your emphasis on avoiding scapegoating and blaming the victim—was very judiciously put. And, of course, your proposal to downsize middle and high schools was beautifully justified on "humane" grounds.

Several things disturbed me during and after the address.

1. It was obvious that Congress was either puzzled or disappointed that you were not promising quick results. Ordinarily, a president's address is interrupted by applause fairly frequently. There were few such interruptions during the "prevention" part of the speech. I am sure they agreed with what you said but they probably were thinking: How would the long-term perspective play with the voters?

2. There was applause for your call to downsize middle and high schools, especially when you emphasized that this would require more construction and personnel, especially in our urban areas. Was it because of what it meant for the economy or because they truly understood that smaller schools were, as you well put it, a necessary but *not* sufficient condition for changing the contexts of learning? Did they hear the "necessary but *not* sufficient" message, i.e., the proposal is no guarantee that the clouds will part and the sun will shine?

3. Why weren't they more responsive to the clear way you presented the big idea? Was it because it *is* a simple idea, or was it they were trying to imagine what the "practical" implications were for classrooms and preparatory programs? It is my opinion that in some inchoate way they sensed that you were truly calling for an educational revolution and that it was unsettling.

4. Congress heard what it was prepared to hear: *new* proposals, *new* directions. But the subdued and relatively infrequent applause suggests that in fact you met their expectations too well. You were forcing them to think in new ways. Few people embrace *their* need to change with gyrations of enthusiasm.

5. You deserve sainthood for your argument against vouchers. It was a masterstroke to distinguish between vouchers and parental choice, i.e., you are not opposed to choice that does not discriminate against low-income families.

> Let me be candid with the congress and the American people. Our primary goal is to change our schools, *all of our schools*, in ways that are a departure from what they now are. Our nation is faced with a choice far more momentous than vouchers or parental choice or national testing or the national certification of teachers. I am not saying that these proposals are completely without merit. What I am saying is that they are at this time a distraction from the real choice: Do we have the courage to forge and implement an educational vision that will transform how educators and our children engage in and experience the learning process? Can we make our schools interesting, stimulating, mind-provoking places where both teachers and students willingly strive for and experience the sense of growth?

That got the applause it deserved, although not at the decibel level I hoped for.

6. The last part of your address got the frequent applause it deserved. In my letters to you I only alluded to the brute fact that what children experience in their families and neighborhoods—especially in our urban areas—too frequently

engender antieducational attitudes in children. To expect that only by radically changing our schools will the problems in living that too many children experience disappear or even dramatically be diluted in their antieducational consequences is asking too much. "Just as a nation we have learned that what happens outside our borders can adversely affect us, it is a lesson we have to learn in regard to what happens outside the walls of our schools. If we—as we should—expect a great deal of our schools, let us remember that the realization of those expectations will require supportive changes outside those school walls." You should give at least a week off to whomever drafted that part of the address.

7. What was most disturbing to me were the panels the TV and cable networks assembled to comment on your address. Each had at least two educational "leaders"—including some past secretaries of education—some congressmen, and, of course, well-known TV journalists. Although all of them said that your address was an outline of your program and that specifics would be embodied in forthcoming legislative proposals, they were either critical or puzzled. Critical because they could not fathom in what ways you wanted classrooms to change, what changes in existing requirements or structure your "philosophy" would entail, what your proposals will do now to stem the downhill course, and, as one "expert" said with the obvious approval of some of the others, "It sounds as if the President is out to resurrect John Dewey as guru." They heard the big idea, they were incapable of understanding it. I take heart that on the panel Esther and I were watching the chairwoman of the house committee on education had the final say: "You people have completely ignored the most obvious and compelling fact in the President's address: Whatever we have tried in the past has not worked. Our intentions were sincere and serious. We hoped and we prayed and we spent money. It didn't get us much. We are worse off than before. The President is pointing us in new directions. His program is a challenge to the way things are. I have heard nothing in this discussion that praises the President for having the guts to say that we have met the enemy and it is us." The panel members looked quite uncomfortable. I would guess they were relieved that there was no time for them to respond.

What that congresswoman said, Mr. President, has to be said daily by you and your congressional leaders. The *New York Times* today had an editorial similar in substance to what the congresswoman said. Let us allow ourselves to hope that your address will garner general support. Of one thing I can assure you: Regardless of what happens, that address ensures you will not be a footnote in the history books. I am sorry I will not be around when those books are written. I do have a vested interest in my batting average.

Our regards to both of you,

Seymour B. Sarason

P.S. Yours was one of those addresses that reads as well as it sounds.

P.S. There are a couple of pet ideas I will unload on you and then I will let you alone!

P.S. Listening to that TV panel last night reminded me that the First Amendment is a mixed blessing. I will still contribute to the ACLU!

XXIX

Dear Mr. President:

This letter is an effort to get you thinking about education other than in terms of school or college populations. As you know, I still want to save the world, all of it! Since I will not have time to do it, I will try to get you to take on the task! I am only being half-facetious when I say that when rescue fantasies are extinguished in people they are in deep, deep trouble. As preface to this particular rescue fantasy I have to tell you about certain events in the immediate post World War II period.

I begin with the GI Bill of Rights, which was powered by several things. The first was the desire of a grateful nation to provide new educational and life-enhancing opportunities to the millions of returning veterans. The second was the memory of the societal dislocation that occurred when veterans returned after World War I. The third, related to the second, was the fear (and it was a fear) that our economy could not absorb millions of returning veterans. The GI Bill had preventive and repair features. What was remarkable, truly remarkable, was the number of veterans who eagerly took advantage of the opportunity to change the direction of their lives. They literally were given new leases on life. In my opinion it was and is scandalous that no one saw fit to study why so many people seized the opportunity and how it affected the rest of their lives. *The GI Bill transformed our society*. That is not an overstatement. What that legislation presented to veterans was this question: How do you want to use education to exploit your interests and dreams, to test and challenge your talents and abilities, again to feel there is a personal world to conquer? What has gone unremarked about the GI Bill is how clear it was that these veterans—

many of whom had established careers and professions—
wanted, needed new experience, a chance to be other than
what they had been. The GI Bill was a magnificent contribution both to lives *and* our society. It was in its own way
testimony to the validity of the big idea: *Start where the*
veterans are, with what they think and want to do, and help them
reintegrate themselves into "our" world.

Back in the late forties (I think) General Eisenhower, who
was then president of Columbia University, got behind a
study by Eli Ginsberg (economist) and Douglas Bray (psychologist) on what happened to soldiers who were recruited
into military service but who, either because of illiteracy or
a low IQ score, should not have been selected. They wrote
a book *The Uneducated.* I plead with you to read the appen-
dix where these soldiers express their gratitude for the *spe-*
cial opportunity the army provided them to learn to read and
write up to a fourth-grade level. They were in a program in
which each was part of a *very small group* who *lived* with
someone (few had teaching credentials) whose job it was to
help them read and write. They could live with that person
for no more than 120 days. If at the end of that time they
could not reach the fourth-grade level, they were to be
released from service. The average time it took most of them
to reach the standard was between 90 and 100 days. When
you read what that experience meant to them, how they
regretted their earlier attitudes toward school and learning,
and how it changed their sense of worthiness, you are almost
ready to cry for joy.

All of the above is by way of saying that there are many
people today *in all walks of life* who feel "slotted," in a rut,
fearful of a future that will not challenge them. Many of
them are highly successful people who yearn for new opportunities to move in new directions.

I am talking about what I have called the "one life-one
career imperative." Our society—especially in the post World
War II era—said to our youth: "You can be many things in
life. You can be A *or* B but you cannot be A *and* B. Choose."
Remember, Mr. President, that was a time when people
expected and were told that a "new world" was in the offing,
one that would not be governed by the traditions of the "old"

one that was responsible for two world wars. People bought the message that they can be many things in life, that they owed it to themselves to experience as much as life had to offer. In the case of millions of veterans that meant they were and should not be bound by what they had been. The GI Bill gave them the opportunity to make a new vocational choice. They seized the opportunity. What that meant for their generation, veterans or not, was significant but more significant was the fact that the message that you can and should be many things in life was transmitted to the next generation. In spades.

Understandably, what no on saw clearly at the time was that the thrust of the message was on a collision course with the one life-one career imperative, i.e., you can be many things in life but, vocationally speaking, you could only be *one* thing. Choose! The psychological dynamics undergirding that message went far beyond the vocational arena, and it was inevitable that that arena would reflect those dynamics, with the consequence that many people would come to resist and resent having to stay within the confines of their vocational choice. However, if only for economic reasons, switching careers was impossible for most people. It was a source of frustration and fading dreams about experiencing what life had to offer.

In my unread book with the unilluminating title *Work, Aging, and Social Change*, I put it this way: *Our society has made it far easier to change marriage partners than to change careers, but their dynamics are identical.* I did not put it that way because I "approved" of those dynamics—I am still uncertain where I stand—but as an observation I thought then and now to be valid.

Put my *explanation* aside. Assume that my explanation is invalid or at best woefully incomplete. The fact remains that too many people in our society are unhappy with the prospect that they will end their lives having been A and not the Bs or Cs in which they would have wanted to challenge themselves. It would be an egregious mistake to assume that these people are dissatisfied with having been A. (My orthopedist, for example, who has been quite successful would like nothing better than to give up his practice and become a medical historian.) I have talked to too many people *in all walks of life*—plumbers, electricians, lawyers, physicians, teachers, business people, tree experts, and (yes) professors—who would seize the opportunity, as so many veterans did, to introduce educational-vocational diversity into their lives. To live the unexamined life is bad enough. To live the unexperienced life has become personally and societally destabilizing for too many people. Indeed, too many people are quite aware that whatever kicks they will get out of life will no longer be from being A.

These ideas may seem strange to you. I can assure you they are not strange to many people in the quiet of their nights.

When we think of education we think about young people in elementary, secondary schools and, of course, in higher education. If that is understandable, if there were times in the past when that restriction in our thinking was deemed sufficient for society's purposes and its self-interests, we had better wake up to the fact that our world has changed in dramatic ways and degrees. Education in its most broad and invigorating sense has truly become a lifelong need in people's lives. At present it is a strong but inchoate need, one which people have difficulty articulating, let alone proclaiming publicly. If we continue to ignore that need, if we do not fathom the ramifications of that need in a world of changed values, perspectives, and purposes, if we continue to ignore the educational desire *and* fantasies of people, we will be contributing to societal dynamics the consequences of which I, for one, do not contemplate happily.

Are these the musings of a crotchety old man? Someone who confuses change with a downhill slide? Someone whose sourness is no less extreme than the obtuse optimism of Voltaire's Dr. Pangloss? My answer would require a book. Since that book will not be written, I give you the most brief of answers: I lived through most of the worst century in human history.

But I did not write this letter to defend myself against *ad hominems*, although I spend a great deal of my days in imaginary arguments with all kinds of people. (I win *all* of the arguments!) I wrote this letter because I now have reason to believe that you truly want to go down in history as the only Education President who was co-equal in purpose and vision with Thomas Jefferson.

Respectfully,

Seymour B. Sarason

P.S. I feel the need to write you and the Third Lady a concluding letter. Not because that is the Emily Post thing to do, although that would be reason enough. I have to understand that need better before I write. If my self-exploration is fruitless, the Emily Post letter will have to suffice.

P.S. I have a peculiar mind. When I wrote the above P.S. I thought of a joke. It's about the ninety-year-old woman who went to her stock broker to seek advice about how she should invest some of her savings. He made a number of suggestions all of which, he emphasized, gave the possibility of quick profits. She listened carefully and when he was through, she said, "I'm afraid I wasn't clear. I want to be in the market for the long term." I now know what I want to say in my concluding letter.

XXX

Dear Dr. Cory:

Although I am most pleased that the President passed on to you my last letter, I must tell you that I had to overcome a good deal of resistance to send it to him. For one thing, I knew that what I wanted to convey I could not clearly, persuasively, compellingly do in a brief letter. Pithiness has never been my long suit. But there was more than that. When back in the late sixties I had my "aha" experience about the dynamics *and* future of the one life-one career imperative, a lot of other observations began to fall into place, not the least of which was the escalating divorce rate, or the number of people I knew or heard who were "dropping out" (Santa Fe was a very popular way station). The country seemed to be on a social cloud chamber that no one could make sense of. In any event, how could I in a letter convey the context from which the one life-one career imperative popped into my head?

The truth is that what "tongue-tied" me in writing the letter was the thought that the President would view my ideas not only as wacky but calculated to destabilize our society quicker and more thoroughly. Apparently, my fears, if not groundless, were not justified.

If I read between the lines of your letter, the President wants *you* to tell him whether my ideas make practical sense. "The president", you wrote, "thought he got the gist of your ideas, especially in relation to the GI Bill part of your letter, but beyond intuitive feeling that what you say has validity, he said he frankly had a blank mind." I am most appreciative that you hied yourself over to the congressional library to get and read my book. I am going to be very frank with you. (At my age I can afford to be frank!) I wish I knew you better so that I would have a secure basis for judging whether to accept your strong words of praise for that book. You say it is one of the best books I have written. My opinion is that it, together with the *Predictable Failure of Educational Reform*, are the best books I have written, using the criterion of the degree to which an idea or book validly explains past and present societal dynamics and predicts their countenance into the future. Yes, it is a shaky criterion!

What, you ask, are the policy implications of what I wrote? My answer is *none at this time* and for two reasons. The first is that the problem has no public currency, i.e., it is not something that has received formulation and discussion pro or con. The second is that we simply do not know the extent to which it is an issue in the lives of people. However certain I may feel that the problem is widespread and its consequences for individuals and the society have been and will continue to have largely (but not exclusively) negative effects, I do not fool myself that I or anyone else has provided a firm basis for the conclusion that it is an important societal problem. There are too many questions for which we need better answers than we now have.

Here are some of the questions:

1. How many people—again in all walks of life and of different periods of adulthood—have found themselves wishing that they could move into a new line of work?

2. How many of these people can say (and how quickly) what that new line of work would be?

3. Among those who would seek a change, what are the different reasons contributing to such seeking? Dissatisfaction with what they have done and are now doing? A felt need to give expression to longstanding or new interests? Improvement of economic status? A sense of lack of challenge, of boredom, of withering on the vine?

4. What have been the obstacles to making the change? Are they only economic? Is it a reluctance or fear to return to "school" if that were necessary? A lack of family or marital support for such a move? What do they consider to be the *minimal* conditions that would enable them to shift? What sacrifices are they prepared to make?

5. Among those who would seek a change, how do they see the personal and interpersonal consequences if they could make that change? If they cannot?

6. Putting vocational change aside, how many people would seek further education simply as a way of satisfying intellectual curiosity and interest? I am not referring, although not excluding, adult education courses in local high schools. I am referring to college courses and programs. (Our plumber comes to mind. He is a high school graduate who would love to take history courses, just history courses, but he assumes that the local college—Yale is out of the question!—would not permit him to do *just* that.) How many people would love to be a student again?

I could go on and on. The questions are many. What needs to be established is how people perceive and experience the consequences of the one life-one career imperative. If I am correct, those consequences are frequently negative in their effects *and*, therefore, both cause and effect of negative societal factors.

A concrete first step. The president should appoint a national commission to study the educational-vocational needs and desires of the adult population. Not a study that starts with preconceptions based on narrow conceptions of education and work, on what has been and is, on preconceptions implicitly suffused by the imagery of the one life-one career imperative. *I am talking about a series of studies that take the big idea as seriously with adults as that big idea should be taken with children: You start with what is in the minds and hearts of people about their ideas, hopes, fantasies, questions.*

I may be all wet. I feel in my bones that I am absolutely correct. If I am, then what I am suggesting is an idea whose time has come, and as long as that idea does not gain currency, we will be at the mercy of forces that are as fateful as they are strong and unrecognized.

What does this add up to? It is not enough to be a president who seriously seeks to improve the education of our youth. An education president should be one of who calls for and fosters an *educational society*, i.e., education for all of its citizens. That is a vision, but it is not visionary.

Where that vision takes us is uncertain. What are first and second steps is less important at this time than getting to the point where we know we have to start stepping.

We are in the twenty-first century. Is there anyone who can look back at the twentieth century without regret that we did not recognize or pay attention to what we *now* know should have been obvious? Yes, I know that hindsight gives us 20-20 vision. But let us not ignore the lesson: Our insensitivity to what should have been obvious in the past is no less true of us in the present. That should make us humble but not resigned to passivity. We should try to do better even if it means that at best we will only glimpse a facet of what the future will say should have been obvious.

Cordially,

Seymour B. Sarason

P.S. I appreciate the "testimony" about your professional career and the one life-one career imperative.

P.S. I have a final letter I will send to the President and the Third Lady. It is not that I do not have more to say but enough is enough. I do not want to wear out my welcome. Besides, regurgitating in any form anything I have written has always been a problem for me. I can listen to myself only so long, and I have had it. To the extent that writing can be enjoyable—which means to the extent that it is a minor form of Chinese torture—I enjoyed writing to the President. I'll quit while I'm ahead. I wish you well. I'll be watching what goes on from a distance but with piercing and hopeful eyes.

XXXI

Dear Mr. President:

I predicted correctly that I would have trouble with this letter. Like the aged lady who invested for the "long term," I wanted our conversation to go on and on. I too was in for the long term. Fortunately, my grip on inexorable reality tells me otherwise. (Why "fortunately"?)

Although I will not be around to see what happens in the long term, I take great satisfaction in the fact that you have started a process as significant for our country as it is overdue. The outcome is uncertain—it always is—but I congratulate you for your courage in trying to change the substance and direction of the educational debate. When I look back over my long life, I find myself asking why things so frequently did not work out as I planned and hoped. At the same time I am aware that I have learned a lot, albeit not as much as I would have wanted. And one of the things I learned is that Lady Luck is a fickle creature. So much depends on the right factors coming together at the right time. When I listened to your campaign speeches, and the public response to your resolve to move in new ways in regard to our schools, I allowed myself to renew my hope that maybe the times were ripe for real change. That's why I began to write to you. If you will go back over my letters, you may see that my hopes were accompanied by some fears, the most crucial of which is that you may underestimate what you are up against. To put it baldly: I feared (and still fear) that as you saw the implications of your goals, and as you would experience a barrage of criticism from those mired in tradition, you would resign yourself to accepting cosmetic changes. As a person of action, you want to see *results*.

What makes this letter so difficult is that I felt I had to tell you that at the end of your presidency (I hope at the end of a second term) you will not be satisfied by *results*. At best, you will take satisfaction from the fact that you changed the substance and direction of the debate. I will never forget the response to President Truman's call for a national health program. It went nowhere. Some said that he was one of our worst presidents. It did not take more than a couple of decades for President Truman to become a political icon for both political parties. All this is by way of saying that your call for radical reform of our schools may meet a similar fate. Why do I say "may"? It *will* meet a similar fate. But part of that fate will be that you forever put some new ideas into public currency. *That is no small feat.* That is what should keep you going. You should judge yourself the way you would want history to judge you, i.e., you had the guts to articulate and to seek to implement new ideas. You fought the good fight.

And what is at the core of that fight? Unless and until we learn how to change how children and teachers experience themselves and each other *in the classroom*—how the big idea should suffuse all that goes on—our schools will remain what they are or get worse. If you start with that goal, it becomes clear what other institutional dominos have to fall. It is unrealistic in the extreme to expect that the dominos will fall quietly. Institutional change engenders turmoil, unless of course, as in the past, the change is cosmetic.

I am repeating myself, and I do not want to wear out my welcome. (I am taking the liberty of enclosing a letter I wrote to Dr. Cory, one of your advisors.) Although there is much more I would want to say to you, I have, wisely I think, restricted myself to a few ideas. You do not need any more ideas from me. By virtue of your message to Congress, you have put ideas into the political process where you are incomparably more knowledgeable than I am. We are told that politics is the art of the possible. But there is art and there is art. I pray that Lady Luck will look upon you favorably so that what becomes possible, if anything becomes possible, will not be a charade covering up defeat. In any event, Mr. President, in my book your first step has put you on the Truman road.

You will have to decide whether I can be of further help to you. Please be assured that as long as I can take pencil to paper I will respond to any question you direct to me.

By responding to my letters, you and the Third Lady have brightened my days in ways I never contemplated. Too frequently in history those who spoke truth to power came to regret it. Far from regretting it, my appreciation has no bounds.

Esther and I send our best wishes to you and the Third Lady. We'll be watching from the sidelines.

Our warmest regards,

Seymour and Esther Sarason
Long-Term Investors